Marcus Katz

Marcus Katz is a professional tarot teacher at the Far Away Centre, a contemporary training centre in the Lake District of England. As the Codirector of Tarot Professionals, the world's largest professional tarot organization, he has studied and taught tarot for thirty years and has delivered more than ten thousand face-to-face readings. His first book, *Tarosophy*, has been termed a "major contribution" to tarot by leading teachers. Marcus is also the cocreator of *Tarot-Town*, the social network for tarot, with more than ten thousand people worldwide sharing innovative tarot development.

Tali Goodwin

Tali Goodwin is the Marketing Director and Cofounder of Tarot Professionals, the largest professional tarot organization in the world. She has coauthored innovative teaching books such as *Tarot Flip*, which is regularly in the top ten best-selling tarot books on Kindle. Tali is a skilled researcher and is credited with bringing the long-hidden Waite-Trinick Tarot to publication in *Abiding in the Sanctuary: The Waite-Trinick Tarot.* She also coedited the leading tarot magazine, *Tarosophist International*, in 2010–2011.

To Write to the Authors

If you wish to contact the authors or would like more information about this book, please write to the authors in care of Llewellyn Worldwide, Ltd. and we will forward your request. The authors and publisher appreciate hearing from you and learning of your enjoyment of this book and how it has helped you. Llewellyn Worldwide, Ltd. cannot guarantee that every letter written to the authors can be answered, but all will be forwarded. Please write to:

Marcus Katz and Tali Goodwin
% Llewellyn Worldwide
2143 Wooddale Drive
Woodbury, MN 55125-2989

Please enclose a self-addressed stamped envelope for reply, or $1.00 to cover costs. If outside the USA, enclose an international postal reply coupon.

MARCUS KATZ
AND TALI GOODWIN

LENORMAND
HANDBOOK

Llewellyn Publications
Woodbury, Minnesota U.S.A.

First Edition
First Printing, 2015

Cover art © 2015
   iStockphoto.com/19159039/©ShutterWorx;
   iStockphoto.com/14202670/©Cloudniners;
   iStockphoto.com/9552473/©Cloudniners;
   iStockphoto.com/5269825/©Cloudniners
Cover design by Kevin R. Brown
Lenormand Oracle Cards used by permission of LoScarabeo

Llewellyn is a registered trademark of Llewellyn Worldwide Ltd.

Library of Congress Cataloging-in-Publication Data (Pending)
ISBN: 978-0-7387-4712-5

Llewellyn Worldwide does not participate in, endorse, or have any authority or responsibility concerning private business transactions between our authors and the public.

   All mail addressed to the author is forwarded but the publisher cannot, unless specifically instructed by the author, give out an address or phone number.

   Any Internet references contained in this work are current at publication time, but the publisher cannot guarantee that a specific location will continue to be maintained. Please refer to the publisher's website for links to authors' websites and other sources.

Llewellyn Publications
A Division of Llewellyn Worldwide Ltd.
2143 Wooddale Drive
Woodbury, MN 55125-2989
www.llewellyn.com

Printed in the United States of America

Contents

Introduction

There was an anchor, an hourglass
surmounted by a skull, a bull, a beehive...
Thirty-six altogether, and she
couldn't even guess what they meant.
—Philip Pullman, *Northern Lights*

Welcome to the world of the Lenormand cards. You have in your hands a simple but powerful deck of fortune-telling cards that is as old as dreams, yet can be applied to everyday modern life. Let us introduce to you the history of these cards and their symbols and then you can get straight to using them to clarify and divine your questions.

In Nuremberg, Germany, around 1799, a new parlour game was created by the son of a wealthy industrialist. J. K. Hechtel invented several such games, even though he was the member of a rich family specialising in brass production, which was in much demand. Nuremberg at that time was also a hotbed of card and dice game production, so Mr. Hechtel was surrounded by publishers and designers of such amusements and diversions.

Many of these games were teaching games as well as fun; they were designed to be seen as educating people in morals and life, not as a means of encouraging gambling. So the new parlour game of Hechtel's was called "The Game of Hope" and was played by laying out thirty-six cards in a sequence and then racing other players using dice, in a manner similar to "Snakes and Ladders." In fact, all such games derive from the earliest known format, "A Game of Goose," and perhaps trace their ancestry even earlier back to the Senet game of ancient Egypt.

The Game of Hope was typical of such games, and used on each card a simple symbol which was instantly recognisable to the European Christians of the time: a dog for faithfulness, a garden park for socialising, a cross for suffering, and an anchor for hope or faith. It also used symbols for the fables which would be told around the dining table or at bedtime; the cunning fox appears from the Reynard stories, and in another card we see the stork eating the frog, showing what happens to frogs who get too big for their pond!

Most of these symbols were already familiar to players and used in a card game (discovered by Mary K. Greer and seen by us in the British Museum) called the Coffee Cards; and these in turn took their symbolism from the common shapes interpreted in coffee grind reading. So, the Coffee Cards made it easy to tell fortunes by shuffling a deck of cards rather than interpreting patterns in the bottom of a coffee cup. Hechtel took that game, tweaked it, and turned it into a parlour game.

Some fifty years later, a noted fortune-teller, Mlle. Lenormand, died in Paris. Whilst we have no clear record of the cards she used in her various ways of telling fortunes, it is likely that they were Piquet cards, a popular everyday card deck in France at the time. However, some enterprising publisher took Hechtel's "Game of Hope," now long after his death, and fastened the name "Lenormand" to it to capitalise on the interest in her upon her death.

The adverts then—and since—have all suggested that you too can read the future as Mlle. Lenormand did, with these, her secret cards! Unfortunately, it is unlikely that she did use these cards, so they only bear her name in a marketing connection rather than in actual use.

Be that as it may, the cards themselves have survived as a means of cartomancy, perhaps because they do indeed go back to the earliest form of divination, reading shapes in coffee grinds, which in turn goes back to reading shapes in nature and in dreams. A snake in a card, in a tea-leaf pattern, in a cloud, in a dream, all symbolise the same thing—danger.

We will take you through every card and its symbolism and you will also learn the literal language of Lenormand; a snake is always a snake, a dog always means a good friend—there are clear negative and positive cards with Lenormand reading. You will soon learn how to put the cards together and listen to the message of the symbols through combinations; the Sun and the House will tell you that you will be lucky staying close to home, or the Sun and the Ship will advise setting sail for better fortune!

However the cards fall, we encourage you to learn this literal language and receive new insights into any situation that you may present to the cards, for yourself or for others.

May the Sun shine, the Moon reflect well upon your House, and the Rider bring you only Clover.

ONE

The Cards

Before we look at individual cards in order, let us first try a little experiment with literal reading of the Lenormand. Shuffle your deck and remove two cards, placing them next to each other.

EXERCISE: READING LITERAL LENORMAND

Say out loud, "[Name of card 1] finds itself next to [name of card 2]."

As an example, we might pull the Lady (29) and the Snake (7) cards. I would say, "The Lady finds herself next to the Snake." Now that will immediately conjure up a particular image and feeling—she should get away from that snake, as it probably means her no good. She may not even see it, because it is so close to her.

Or we could pull the Dog (18) and the Anchor (35) cards. This sounds immediately like the name of an English pub, "The Dog and Anchor." So we say, "The Dog finds itself next to the Anchor." What does this bring to mind? We get the idea that the dog is standing by the anchor, perhaps waiting for a ship. Perhaps the dog is guarding it. What do you think it might mean?

You can repeat this exercise for two or more cards. With three cards, you can say out loud, "(Card 2) finds itself between (card 1) and (card 3)." Really stick to the literal image of the cards before going into the meanings below. We have all been in a situation that could be described as "the Child finds itself between the House and the Garden." It is wonderful how literal and direct the Lenormand cards can be if you allow them to speak clearly and simply.

Once you have mastered a few horizontal arrangements of two or more cards, you can work on vertical arrangements.

Lay out two cards, the second below the first, and say, "[Card 2] is below [card 1]." This might be as simple as "the Dog is below the Whip," which would need hardly any interpretation, or slightly more obscure such as "the Sun is below the Tower." In this latter case, perhaps we might sense that the day is late for the situation, and whatever authority or power the Tower had is now diminished. Try saying it the other way around: "The Tower is above the Sun." What sense might that make?

Once you have practised a few arrangements for yourself, let us now introduce each card with its main meanings for your reference.

1. The Rider

We begin at the beginning with the Rider; he is the carrier of news, the messenger, who can herald change in your life. This card can be indicative of an actual person of influence coming into your life. The Rider card traditionally brings good news; something of importance you have been anticipating

Figure 1. The Rider

and waiting on will come about. The positive influence of the Rider can be negated by the cards around it; for example, the Rider followed by the dark shadow edge of the Cloud is the ominous delivery of bad news. It is a warning of bad influence entering the sitter's life. Literally speaking, this is saying, "The Rider brings dark clouds." All is not doom and gloom in the Lenormand; this combination can have some light thrown on it by the appearance of the Sun card. Take a look at how the following can foretell "sun after rain":

- The Rider + The Clouds + The Sun literal reading:
  The Rider brings dark clouds, followed by the sun.

If this card is all about you, there is an emotional imperative that you are not acting upon, where action needs to be taken. You need to express how you feel and stop dragging your heels; you can only do this by moving onward. However, it is important to keep your poise and centre or you could be easily thrown off your course. As a general interpretation, this could involve receiving a visitor who has some good news to impart.

2. The Clover

This is the card of luck, as seen traditionally, and as discussed earlier in this chapter. We take it as being fortunate, as being given a "little luck," and a positive card in a reading. It is an encouragement to try something new, or to receive (particularly when combined with the Bouquet) an offer of assistance.

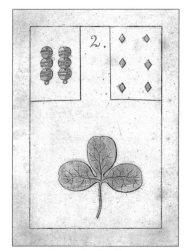

Figure 2. The Clover

In financial situations, it is a card of lucky returns or a good investment, depending on the surrounding cards. The obvious and literal meaning of a House card, a Clover card, and a Heart card needs no explanation! If you add the Gentleman and the Ring, and present the Lady card, no doubt you would expect the Child card to follow!

This card is a reassurance that all is well, and that the situation you are in is secure and will bring peace of mind. You can relax and spend time enjoying this security. Treat yourself and be kind to yourself—you deserve the best.

This card says for you to keep positive; you are in for some good luck and great abundance.

3. The Ship

The Ship is a signifier of travel and movement. This card can signify potential and opportunities out there. If there is a situation or project you have been wary of acting upon, now is the time to set sail and embrace the change and progress that will be yours. Have you found yourself settling into a mundane routine? If so,

Figure 3. The Ship

you need to make changes, think about where you see yourself in the future. It is never too late to do the things we have been putting off!

Moving on, the conditions are perfect and the timing is right to move forward. The journey will require a certain amount of skill as you navigate onward, plotting through difficult conditions to ensure a safe passage. Harness the power of natural resources; the wind brings change and movement—do not shy away from making the changes. A new life could be yours!

The ship is a very favourable card and takes us to a good place.

4. The House

The House in the Lenormand is sanctuary, security, and most of all "home, sweet home," which gives it a very positive context. It is shelter from the turmoil of the outside world and signifies familiarity. However, as with all the Lenormand cards, its positive aspect can be influenced negatively by the following combinations:

Figure 4. The House

- The Whip + House = Strife in home

- The Fish + Whip + House = Money-related strife in home

- The Anchor + House + Key + Snake = Stable home open to threat

This last combination is a warning to beware of snakes at your door. Take care not to invite anyone into your inner sanctum you cannot trust.

Consider the saying "home is where the heart is." This card is one of stability and strength, an indicator of a good life, the perfect combination of family contentment and emotional well-being accompanying it. If this card appears in relation to a query on making a commitment to a relationship that has come into your life, the card is optimistic that there is healthy compatibility.

5. The Tree

This card is all about tradition, lineage, and ancestor wisdom, the wisdom of the ages that stands the test of time. Think of the enormous life span of a tree, such as the Methuselah Tree, which is thousands of years old, and has stood solid and strong through many changes that have brought famine, war, and turmoil. It has seen all

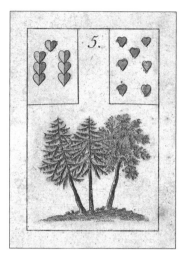

Figure 5. The Tree

around it alter for good and bad, man has encroached upon its sacred space, but still it maintains its dignity. It has staying power; this card is advising you too to have staying power. The Methuselah Tree is known to have a survival strategy that has enabled it to do this; it "spreads its roots and expands its crown," and to make the most of the resources it absorbs to survive.

Take a leaf from this old tree, and do not bend and give up when all around you is out of control; reconnect to the wisdom that is within you, the wisdom that has been passed down through your own family tree from your ancestors. Honour them and they will honour you.

6. The Clouds

The Clouds card in the Lenormand is traditionally a
harbinger of uncertainty. It
could also indicate a state of
confusion, of thoughts and
emotions, air and water. We
all have heard of someone
who walks around "with
their heads in the clouds"—
they are in a state of mental
and emotional detachment
that makes them unable to

Figure 6. The Clouds

see what is really going on in a situation. The confusion of
the Clouds cards could be lent some clarity, if it was placed
in close proximity to the Sun card, especially directly above it.
The sun would burn the clouds away.

The shading around the edge of the cloud card can also
point out if the uncertainty is moving towards the sitter or away
from them.

A cloudy sky can portend good or bad weather. When we
see dark and angry clouds in the sky, we are made aware of
bad weather coming our way, and we prepare our day accordingly. This card then is very much about being aware of what is
going on in our environment and reading and acting upon the
signs that we see. The image on the card usually depicts cumu-

lus clouds, dark and light. This could say there will be change ahead, good and bad equally. This card can then imply that the time is right for issues that have been brewing to be brought out into the open, dissipating the pressure that has built up.

7. The Snake

The Snake card stands for a significant other person in the sitter's life, usually a woman, and usually up to no good. This is in part due to the biblical association of the snake with Eve's temptation. There is certainly cause for concern if the Snake card is found lying (literally) underneath the sitter's card.

Figure 7. The Snake

"Take care where you step." The Snake is strong but silent, stealthy, and ready to strike when least expected. It warns us to be ready for the unexpected. If this card makes itself known with regard to relationships, it could signify that somebody may find themselves drawn into a highly sexual and magnetic entanglement.

On a more abstract level, this is a card that favours regenerative healing. If it turns up in response to health, things bode well. Be strong, discreet, and cautious, and especially take care to respect the confidentiality of others.

There is no other way to begin the interpretation of the Snake card than with a pantomimed hiss, and there is no getting away from the fact that the Snake is seen as trouble.

When used as a person card in the Lenormand, the Snake expresses negative character traits, such as being manipulative and slippery by nature. Traditionally it could signify the presence of a jealous woman, a rival in love in the equation. There is betrayal here.

8. The Coffin

Traditionally the Coffin is symbolic of loss through ill health and death. However, one must remember that when the cards were first devised, illness and death played a brutal hand. You would be considered fortunate to live to the age of forty. Women frequently died in childbirth and infant mortality was high. The attitude to illness

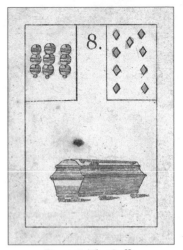

Figure 8. The Coffin

and death was one of reconciliation; it was something people of the time were quite understandably very preoccupied about.

So what does the Coffin really mean? It can literally be the "end" of something such as a relationship or marriage, money problems, a job, hardship and strife, being taken for granted, or even the end of your travels.

The card also reminds us of ritual farewell, the end of an era, acceptance of something being done and finished, adopting a way of being that accepts the inevitable, or out-worn regrets needing to be put aside. This is the card of initiation, shedding old attachments, and learning to be less egotistical. Await the rebirth of a new you. With regard to timing, completion is near. However, there could be a sense of mourning or sadness at the prospect of change.

9. The Bouquet

Traditionally the Bouquet symbolises joy being presented into one's life. You will receive a token of appreciation that will make you happy, one that could take you by surprise. In the past, flowers were used as a secret code to relay a person's intentions to another in their life, especially of a romantic

Figure 9. The Bouquet

nature. The different combinations in a bouquet of flowers spoke in a Lenormand-like way in a special coded message. We must remember that hidden symbols were very much in the psyche of the people of the day. In the so-called language of flowers, we would see the iris, red rose, and ivy together mean a messenger (iris) of passion (rose) and fidelity (ivy).

"Say it with sentiment or not at all." A sign/expression of appreciation, it could be for romantic considerations or merely for services rendered. Take care to express how much you value a thing or individual in your life; have you a special occasion or celebration coming up? This card is a reminder of being alive and aware of nature's simple beauty, and taking time to "smell the flowers." It could be advising you to take a simplistic, natural approach to gaining that certain somebody's affections;

avoid the materialistic way (leave the Caribbean trip till later). A thoughtful act may bring about positive changes. Feminine energy is swirling. If clarity is needed with regard to a venture or project, good dividends will be rewarded after your work is done.

10. The Scythe

Traditionally in the Lenormand, the card of the Scythe cuts and clears; it is an indication that something will be cut out of your life, and will be no more. It may come as a shock. However this clearing is not all negative, as it will allow the growth of something new. It could be a new lease on life. This can be in regard to a relationship; the

Figure 10. The Scythe

heartbreak of the end of a relationship opens you up to new opportunities, and you may have the chance to meet somebody new. If this is applied to work, the loss of a job can lead to you reassessing your life and the taking up of a whole new career.

"A blunt blade makes work." This card speaks of a call to action and to be prepared for the work ahead. That very thing you have been delaying will soon manifest and will need dealing with before it gets out of hand. Do not underestimate the work involved and what you will be up against. This card's appearance in a layout draws attention to the cards around it, highlighting timing; it can be an indicator of a need for expediency. Placed next to the Snake, for instance, it could be saying to act as soon as possible to confront an individual who has been quietly devious. If the Scythe is placed to the left-hand side, hold back, take a more logical approach, try to reason. If on the right-hand side, confront in a more emotional way.

11. The Whip

A card of trouble, bad words being spoken, unrest, and argument. In some cases it can signify service.

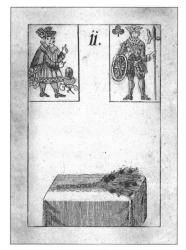

Figure 11. The Whip

"No pain, no gain." This is a card that heavily emphasises the importance of motivation and discipline resulting in achieving our goals. There are ways and means of making progress, and they rarely involve an easy route to success. We have to master our own weakness and turn it into strength to serve us in our endeavours. The ancient Egyptians associated the whip with the emblem of power; therefore this card speaks heavily of self-mastery. Additionally are there areas of our life that we need "whipped into shape"; if so, this card is saying "get to it!" If this card is placed next to the Scythe, this is a double whammy.

The Whip can bring strife and disagreements. There may be a battle for somebody in the relationship either at home or at work to maintain the upper hand, the "whip hand." Such a power struggle in a relationship could manifest as a difficult boss, and the card that embodies this is the Bear. Also be very wary if this card appears in close proximity to the Snake—betrayal could be in the cards.

In a very literal sense, a reprimand is on the way. You may have to pay for some past transgression. The whip is a hard task master that commands discipline. The traditional meaning of the card is strife and disharmony, and it indicates that turmoil will be "whipped up." If the discord is at work, it could mean that morale is at a low, and back-biting and disagreements are making the environment a very unhappy one indeed. This card could also indicate that something or somebody is being whipped up into a frenzy. It could speak to a need to control things in your life.

12. The Birds/ The Owl

The Birds card signifies conversation, communication, and chatter.

"Age-old wisdom, being awakened when others are asleep." This card conjures up Alfred Hitchcock's *The Birds*, especially the scene where the heroine looks out to see the birds that have lined up on the wires. This

Figure 12. The Birds

was very much a metaphor of communication—are we getting the message? If you think about this a little bit deeper and look at it from the view of the original short story by Daphne du Maurier, this story was about the danger of not being in tune with the natural order of things, being spoilt by technology.

This card is saying "listen to your intuition," that which comes naturally and is not forced. The law of correspondence works on all levels. Block out the external noise, and listen to the wise one, the hidden, and the sacred. See beyond, starting from within.

In modern use, this is the card of chatter, gossip, backchat, and real-time communications (unlike the Letter). The card is full of buzz being passed along the grapevine from one person to another.

The Birds means that news spreads fast (particularly with the Rider), via telephone, text message, Facebook, and of course—Twitter.

Where the Birds card appears, everything close to it is already in the air or being broadcast; there is no stopping it.

13. The Child

The Child card literally represents a child in the sitter's life or, at a symbolic level, a childlike nature. This is innocence and play-power.

Figure 13. The Child

"First tentative steps into the world—a living legacy." True honesty, integrity, pure heart, being nonjudgemental and authentic, this is a state of being untainted by cynicism and bitterness. Make a fresh start; it is never too late to learn new things. Be part of new experiences, cast aside the fear that holds you back, go for childlike abandonment. Have trust in the process; those first tentative steps are only just the beginning. The focus for relationships is to be more trusting, authentic, and to come from the heart, not the head.

In a work-related question, this card will show that spontaneity and fresh ideas are needed.

14. The Fox

The card of cunning and trickery, something is always afoot when the Fox is in play. The position of this card in a reading will dictate whether it is you who must be wary, or if others are already out-foxing you. Either way, it is a call to prick up your ears.

The Fox is the entre-preneur of the Lenormand deck; he does not miss a

Figure 14. The Fox

trick, and in fact he is ready to play a trick at any time. The qualities of the fox are quick-wittedness and dexterity in avoiding taking the flack in any situation, especially so at work.

We all know a Mr. (or Ms.) Fox in the workplace; he is full of good ideas, innovation, and has an attitude of self-preservation in life. He is the one waiting to take your promotion when your back is turned, and he will always take the last slice of cake on the plate. All in all, this sort of behaviour has given him a lousy reputation, and he has a good few enemies in life and in the workplace.

The Fox possesses energies you either love or hate, and when he is in a position of influence in your reading, you may be a little wary of what he is up to! However, remember that he's not all bad, and if you put the Fox with Clover for example, it could be foretelling "innovative ideas that come up lucky."

15. The Bear

The Bear is a symbol of power and authority. It can stand for a male figure of stature in the sitter's life, such as a boss. It can also, when combined with the Lady, signify the Mother, and the Gentleman, the Father.

Figure 15. The Bear

In alchemy, the Bear corresponds to nigredo, a blackening process. Therefore this would indicate a cruel and crude energy at play in a situation that is plaguing the sitter. This entanglement could result in primitive instincts being awoken, the sitter or somebody around them being quick to anger, or a situation that could easily become troublesome if not handled with care.

Be wary of not expressing your dark shadow, for as Walt Kelly so wisely wrote, "We have met the enemy, and he is us." The most we have to fear is that which lurks within.

The Bear can be symbolic of business and finance—take for example, a "bear market" in share trading, where when the value of stocks is down, which is seen by some in finance as an opportunity to take advantage by buying up shares when they are at a low, later selling when a profit can be made.

16. The Star

Figure 16. The Star

The Star is the possession of clarity in all things near and far, and a longing for hope and wishes to come true. It is vital to maintain a positive outlook in work-related ventures. Be aware that just because something looks desirable, appearing to offer abundance, big and brash as it may be, do not take for granted that in reality it is so. In astronomy, it is known that the brightest, largest stars are the ones running out of fuel.

The Star card advises us that we need to assess our lives; are we living at too fast a pace, are we too driven to be brighter and better than others at the expense of our own well-being? If we apply the science of a star to ourselves, we are, like the star, at risk of burning out too soon, using up fuel too rapidly in order to maintain our brightest appearance. Remember to plan for the long game!

In general readings, the Star is a card of clarity and vision, blessed with a destination in mind. Follow that which inspires you, do not live life without a sense of purpose, and do not let yourself stray from your destiny.

17. The Stork

The presence of this card in a reading indicates deliverance from a difficult situation, or the delivery of good productive news. The Stork was believed to have significance to the Romans, who considered it a symbol of filial piety.

Figure 17. The Stork

Within the Lenormand, the Stork may speak of the delivery of good or bad news, influenced by the cards in its proximity. The news could materialise in many ways, the most obvious one being the news of a birth. There is an emphasis on a strong family or friendship, one that may imply that your family and friends will be there for you; they can be relied upon in a time of need, and this help could come in the form of a gift.

On the other hand, you may find yourself in a situation where the presence of the Stork may mean you receive news of something being taken away from you for someone else's benefit. For example, you could receive news that you will have to find new accommodation because your landlord is moving his family into the apartment. If the Tree, House, and Scythe appear too, the influence is stronger.

Any reading will make more sense if we look at the character of the Stork; it has a reliable reputation and it will return each year to the place where it has always nested. The Stork is known in the Hebrew language as *chasidah*, the "faithful one." She is one who will always come back, and it is interesting that the word "chasidah" also relates to the Hebrew *chesed*, which for those of you who have some knowledge of Kabbalah means "loving kindness." The stork is known to naturally show acts of kindness toward its fellow storks by its propensity to gift food. However, this behavior is of a selective nature—the stork steals food from other species of birds to fulfil this "kind" act!

18. The Dog

The Dog symbolises loyalty, dependency, and the presence in your life of a trusty friend or loved one. This is the person in the sitter's life who gives unconditional love, but may be a little overly needy. In a more negative way of reading, is there a certain somebody you have welcomed into your life who may end up biting the

Figure 18. The Dog

hand that feeds them? There is a need to take charge and let others know you are top dog!

The dog is a faithful companion who coexists naturally with humans yet still maintains a primal nature. Dogs are able to make the best of both worlds—primal and domestic. If you look after a dog well, it will reward you with endless attention and an open, loving heart. However, the dog is a pack animal: it needs to know its place in the pack, otherwise it takes leadership, thinking you are of a lower rank.

When combined with workplace or authority cards, this card can bring to our attention issues of hierarchy and group in-fighting.

19. The Tower

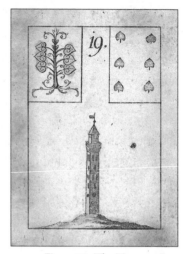

Figure 19. The Tower

The Tower indicates a need to be aware of what is going on around you, to be ready for any eventuality. It is true that forewarned is forearmed. This card is saying you have the upper ground; you are in a good position to ensure that your security is safe and sound. The Tower is the place to be—you find yourself in an elevated position. This is a card of caution, expressing the importance of maintaining higher ground in a situation.

This card could speak of an overly defensive stance that could leave you well-protected but out of favour. If this card appears in relation to a health issue, it could be indicative of the immune system's defensive role. It could also indicate the need to withdraw physically as well as emotionally from other people in order to rest and recuperate.

From another perspective it can be about the need to look beyond the present situation we are in to project our situation into the long term. We need to be more analytical and more objective in our planning, maybe even strategic. If the Ring followed the Tower, it would be saying, "Plan and survey before committing yourself to a contract." A signet ring would apply the seal to the deal! In combination with the Letter card, the need to be sure of the situation before going ahead is consolidated.

The Tower can speak of power and bureaucracy and having to face something far greater than ourselves. We may find ourselves up against a well-established system that is unyielding and seemingly uncompromising. It could manifest itself in the form of a tax department. If we are protected by the system, we become part of the machine itself.

20. The Garden

The Garden card is about getting out into the world and being social in some capacity. It is the card of networking, sharing, and coming together with like-minded people. In the matter of romantic relationships, this could indicate a romantic date or a place with other people such as a party or a meal out.

Figure 20. The Garden

More generally, the card, particularly in the French tradition, tends to signify a "natural life," a life of cultured appreciation. It is often pictured with a fountain, which nourishes one's capacities to enjoy life, and in return is nourished. If this card appeared in a workplace situation, it would indicate that all would run smoothly and harmoniously, even creatively.

It could be indicative of marriage and union, especially when close to the Ring, which is about pledge and commitment. Throw in the Heart and Clover, and it may be a marriage made in heaven, though it will take effort and dedication to maintain, just like the loving care and work put into nurturing flowers and plants in a garden.

The Snake close to the Garden literally speaks of lies and betrayal lurking in a social environment. This is a reflection of the story of Eden, however in mundane terms it is a workplace or the world of social media: Facebook, Twitter. We know that not all news is good news, and a Snake and Garden combination warns of being manipulated by others who only have their own best interests at heart.

Be heartened if the Stork is close by; it could ease the situation. Storks are known predators of the Snake, so their proximity can negate a malicious situation.

21. The Mountain

Figure 21. The Mountain

"Don't make a mountain out of a molehill." The Mountain can represent an obstacle or a diversion. When attempting to reach a goal or commitment, we sometimes have to surmount various challenges. A particularly difficult blockage or obstacle can tempt us to retreat, but the context of this card will tell us if retreat is best or if we should find some other way to get over it. Invariably, the best line of action is to grit our teeth, head on up, plant our metaphorical flag, and get to the other side.

The Mountain is also a symbol of durability and the might needed to withstand life's constant wear and tear. The Mountain is seen in some traditions as representing the structure of bones, i.e., the bones of the earth. In relation to health, this could point to rigidity and being inflexible. It could relate to issues with the spine.

If the Mountain card is placed alongside the Mice, an obstacle that may once have seemed great and insurmountable will be put into perspective, and the problem will be seen for what it is. This is especially so if the problem is related to a verbal obstacle or a stubborn situation, where neither party is prepared to give way. There may have been a falling out or words spoken that were threatening and have caused fear.

If you ask the Lenormand about your lack of progress in your career and the Mountain appears close by your significator, it is confirming that you have an obstacle to overcome. However, what you really want to know is how you can overcome this obstacle to progress. If the Mountain is followed by the Mice, it is telling us to carry on gnawing away and producing results. Combined with the Moon it signifies "recognition" and if those are then followed by the Bouquet and the Fish, it would denote that appreciation is due in the form of money.

The Mountain can speak of the need to rise above where you are at the moment. You need to be elevated, and you may find yourself elevated above others, maybe in the promotional sense. New, lofty heights will be reached, but only with struggle.

22. The Ways

"Where there is a will, there is a way." The Ways card is symbolic of choices and decisions to be made as we make our way through life. This card can indicate that you have reached this point in your life, and that now is the time to act. It can speak of a dilemma, a problem that is difficult to solve, or times when you simply cannot get

Figure 22. The Ways

to the crux of the matter. This card when in a place of influence in a reading is summoning the enquirer to exert their will to find a way forward.

When we consider a Lenormand card as indicating somebody's character (for example, when a card appears above or below their significator in a Grand Tableau), then we would see this card as showing an erratic character. It literally indicates somebody always on the move, yet never knowing their destination. It can also be (in one German tradition) a sceptic. Certainly it is somebody we cannot pin down to one place. If it were found in combination with the Ship, it might indicate someone with itchy feet, and with the Anchor it would show someone afflicted with unfulfilled wanderlust.

The Ways is reflective of its own nature in a reading; it is influenced by the cards around it, thus it could indicate willpower, bravery, and courage to follow one's way in the world (if combined, say, with the Bear, the Ship, or the Heart). Combined with the Child, the Tree, the House, or the Mountain, however, it might indicate someone who prevaricates, it is neither one thing nor another, and cannot be found to make a fixed decision.

23. The Mice

This card is negative, and it warns of missing details whilst being distracted by the big picture. Those mice are already eating away at your resources, your confidence, whatever they're nearby. If it's the Ship, for instance, your holiday plans may be unravelled by missing one piece of essential detail (tickets, anyone?).

Figure 23. The Mice

In a professional or family context, the Mice card shows that people we have recently come to know may be nibbling away at our position. If combined with or in proximity to the Snake or the Fox, then this is certainly a warning card. We would look to the Bear to see how our authority could be maintained in this war of the animals!

The Mice also indicate loss, lack of resources, and poverty. In modern parlance, this might be "limiting beliefs," but we see the literal Lenormand as just that—whatever the cause, psychological or spiritual, the result is the same: you are not going to be able to afford to attend that retreat centre if the Mice are not run out of the House. If the Mice are close to the House, it may even indicate a theft of some kind, in traditional usage.

The Mice card possesses the energy of productivity and doing tasks in bite-sized pieces. The mouse is a tiny little thing but is capable of infesting a whole house in no time at all without you even knowing about it. This card in a position of influence could be drawing attention to something going on in your environment you are not managing. You may be letting little things overwhelm you, so much so that you are going to be left with an out of control situation. Come down from that chair of avoidance and fear so you won't be a mouse in your own house!

24. The Heart

The Heart of course speaks for itself; it is a symbol close to us all. When this card is heavily prominent in a reading, it is all about love, relating, and creating a union of some sort, especially when close to the Ring, the Garden, and the Clover.

Figure 24. The Heart

We tend to look at the Heart's situation between the Gentleman and Lady cards to indicate the nature of a relationship, if such is the question asked. We would obviously prefer the heart to be the only card between the two people in relationship! Truly, every three out of five questions you will be asked as a sybil will be of this nature.

In a question with regard to a profession, this card would signify to us that someone is looking well upon the sitter, that they are a likely supporter and sponsor on an emotional and connected level, rather than simply a logical or practical one. The combination of the Bear (power), Tower (authority), and Heart (harmony), would show us a very passionate and powerful workplace.

When the Heart is around other positive cards, its influence is magnified; here it truly shines as the centre of attention—our emotional world is fully satisfied. However, if it is drawn close to negative cards, particularly a majority, rather than "tempering" the cards, as we might be tempted to do in proactive tarot reading, it unfortunately and literally indicates that the heart will be open to negativity. Thus the sitter will experience suffering as a result, more so than if the heart were not in that position.

Generally speaking, in all traditions, the Heart is a peaceful symbol of harmony, whether between two companies in a merger, siblings, romantically involved people, or the result of a court case. The Heart stands for equality and satisfaction.

25. The Ring

The Ring is symbolic of making a commitment, a pledge, and forging a bond. It can relate to love and marriage, matters of work, contracts, and business generally. As with the Heart card, we would look to the Ring and its position between the Gentleman and Lady cards to denote the nature of a re-lationship in terms of com-

Figure 25. The Ring

mitment. If the Ring and the Heart were found only behind the Lady, and the Gentleman was rather close to a Snake, we would have a very recognisable situation. If his card, the Ring, and the Tower were all close together with the Bear or the Fox (if self-employed), he may be wedded to his job too much. Of course, this applies to the Lady card also.

However, this card could be looked at as if somebody is stuck in a situation where they feel that somebody else is "running rings" around them. This goes hand in hand with the traditional image of a ring expressing the commitment of marriage or betrothal, but in a negative view it can be seen as being a habit that is difficult to break.

The sitter could find him- or herself in a situation from which they are having difficulty extricating themselves, such as being unable to get out of a contract they have signed. However, if the sitter asks about signing a business contract, this card followed by the Anchor, Clover, and Bear speaks of a commitment to a secure, successful (lucky), and powerful business.

As an example of how the Lenormand cards can be interpreted in a health reading, the German reader Iris Treppner sees this card in such a reading as indicating a family bind, something about an illness being connected to the family or environment.

26. The Book

The Book is a card of secrecy and knowledge. If your deck has the book "open" then perhaps it indicates more about knowledge and revelation. If it is "closed" then it depicts more of the hidden nature of knowledge. Some readers use the direction in which the book is "open" to read what knowledge is being disclosed. As an example, if the book was drawn

Figure 26. The Book

with the spine to the left of the image, and the card to the right was the Child, then it would indicate a childhood secret or old secret about to come out into the open.

This is a card of learning and using the imagination to go beyond what we know. A book of fiction can transport us to a whole new world where we can experience life beyond our wildest dreams. Nonfiction book can teach skills ranging from the most mundane to the totally way-out—basket-weaving to accessing the secrets of the universe. The Book is power and a ticket to liberty, bringing learning, and learning brings freedom. Therefore, it is a key to unlocking ourselves, particularly when combined, obviously, with the Key.

The influence of the Book in a reading can be a prod to learn something or become better informed. There is something you should know—cards around it would tell you where that knowledge may be obtained: the Tower, for example, would be a school or institution; the Fox, someone with natural ability in the subject of interest.

The Book in close proximity to the Birds and the Rider card says that you should look out for signs (Birds) and the arrival of news (in the form of the Rider) that will inform you of something of which you should be aware.

27. The Letter

The Letter signifies to us the written word. It is thus a literal card of connecting in a concrete manner, be it email or any other written form. In the French tradition, it is a card signifying invitations, such as to a dance or party. If received for an employment question, it would indicate at least a response, the cards around it indicating the nature of the response—the

Figure 27. The Letter

Sun and Moon being positive in this respect, for example, the Mountain and Ways being a resounding negative.

The Letter is a card that literally puts pen to paper, a form of communication and expression that requires considerable care and sentiment. There is something quaint, old-fashioned, and almost precious about letter writing. It calls up images of bygone times when the world was a much smaller and slower place. A letter would be the only way of keeping friends and loved ones informed of your life.

This card expresses the importance of communication, especially the formal written kind. Close to the Ring, it symbolises a contract, whereas next to the Birds or the Rider, it could signify email.

On the negative side, this card modified by the Fox or the Snake could mean difficulty in the fine print of things, particularly if joined by the Mice.

28. The Gentleman

The Gentleman in the reading can be the male Significator or the significant other of
the female sitter. In a wider
sense, it is a sitter's brother,
father (combined with the
Bear), or close male friend
(combined with the Dog).

A few readers use the
court cards of the tarot on the
Lenormand cards to indicate
people and their relationship

Figure 28. The Gentleman

to each other. We cover this in our courses, as it probably would
require a book in itself given the possible combinations and
different schools of reading playing cards.

It can also be symbolic of forceful male energy. This could
indicate the need to be more assertive in a situation, or be
even less so; say for example if a sitter asks advice on how to
deal with a situation where they feel they are being taking
advantage of in some way, causing anger and temptation to
confront the aggressor. If the Gentleman card is behind the
Scythe, it may mean that the sitter needs to "cut" the aggres-
sive behavior.

29. The Lady

The Lady in the reading can be the female significator or the significant other of the male sitter. In a more general sense, it is the sitter's sister, mother, or close female friend (particularly combined with the Dog). If combined with the Child, it is obviously a younger lady.

Figure 29. The Lady

As with the Gentleman card, the Lady is given more detail by surrounding cards. A Lady close to the Garden and the Birds is someone who enjoys social gatherings and gossip. A Lady close to the Bear and Tower may have issues with authority, and so on.

At a more abstract level, it can also be symbolic of nurturing feminine energy in a situation, an energy which needs to be applied to resolve a problem.

30. The Lily

We find the Lily one of the strangest cards in the Lenormand for its symbolism, as it can range from the sacred to profane. It can represent purity or sex, it can represent a good spirit or passion. In effect, it is a placeholder for the whole range of virtue.

The Lily card in a reading can symbolise fertility, or pure and virtuous intent.

Figure 30. The Lily

If the question posed is regarding someone's integrity, the Lily could imply "virtuous intent" followed by the Heart, which is symbolic of love and union, or "all will be well" if followed by the (lucky) Clover.

31. The Sun

The Sun is a highly positive card in Lenormand readings, and predicts success in our work, particularly after effort (Scythe), struggle (Cross), obstacles (Mountain), or troubles (Mice). The Sun can radically turn a reading into a positive situation when it appears at the end of a line of cards. It shines, saying it will all be worth it.

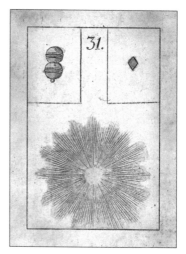

Figure 31. The Sun

So, here comes the sun! The Sun is the life-giver and provider of warmth and well-being. In a reading it symbolises growth on all levels and maintaining a positive face to the world; it promotes confidence and willpower. The Sun's influence in a reading is its ability to throw light on a situation. Next to the Moon card, it is indicative of perfect balance. If these cards are on either side of the Heart card in relation to a question about emotional well-being, this is very good indeed.

The Sun and Moon on either side of the Fish is indicative of a good balance with money, finances, and resources. The Sun above the Garden is good for nurturing growth. The Sun as a timing card is a year.

In a professional context, the Sun indicates advancement and recognition, although again with the Moon, it would provide prediction of a publically recognised advancement. The Sun is a pat on the head, while the Moon is a round of applause.

32. The Moon

The Moon is symbolic of emotions and creativity. It can also represent the idea of letting ourselves be carried away by dreams and fancy. The Moon followed by the Mice can indicate the presence of an emotional obsession that has become repetitive (Mice), rather like the constant chewing of nails—a symptom of some other stress.

Figure 32. The Moon

We are heavily influenced by the Moon itself, from the ebb and flow of the tides cycles, to the influence it exerts on our physical and emotional states. In regard to an enquiry on a relationship issue, the combination of the Heart, Moon, and Clouds together can indicate that the Heart is heading toward emotional change (Clouds). It certainly sounds like an emotional storm is up ahead for our sitter. The Moon can be used as a timing card, indicating a period of twenty-eight days, or around a month.

This is also a card of needing recognition and appreciation. Such a state is highly reactive and always results in constantly looking around to see what others are doing or thinking. Worries of being unable to exert enough influence on others may follow.

33. The Key

The Key denotes opportunity, a figurative unlocking of a situation, although some may read it as a locking up also. To receive the Key and the Heart, for example, means a literal unlocking of the heart by someone, whereas the Book and the Heart might signify someone keeping themselves closed off from you. In the latter case, they are a "closed

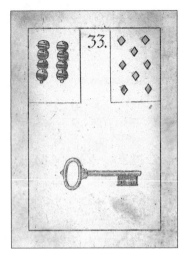

Figure 33. The Key

book" to you, emotionally. The Key and the Ways cards together provide opportunity and choice.

The Key is symbolic as a tool for unlocking something that is closed to you. In times of old, a certain status of authority was attached to the key. The lady of the house would be given the keys to all the doors of the house for safekeeping. In a reading regarding moving house and security, the Key card followed by House then Clover indicates the opening (Key) of the new property (House) will be secure and content (Clover).

The Key can also be symbolic of unlocking knowledge. In a reading, it can confirm that something will be unlocked, and you will be able to make sense of something that has until now puzzled you; you'll have a "Eureka!" moment. In a reading with a question similar to "Will I be able to sort out my current problems and have a peace of mind?" one might receive it as a positive response; the Ways "dilemma" unlocked by the Key, followed by the Star, would indicate the bringing of clarity to the situation.

34. The Fish

The Fish card is symbolic of money and good fortune. It is a literal symbol of resources that can be drawn upon and used in plenty to "feed the people," as was told in the biblical parable. Sometimes in a reading this can represent time as a resource, or other capital. For example, as combined with the Moon in a business situation, this card would represent good will or the recognition of ability as a resource.

Figure 34. The Fish

The Fish announce a change in the tide, bringing a realisation of projects, particularly those with material results. In a reading relating to emotions and relationships, they can indicate the relationship's almost playful nature (or person whose card they affect), seeking joy in life through being with a partner.

In a more psychological interpretation, the Fish swim in the depths of the unconscious, so they represent hidden desires, feelings, and deeper currents. In a Grand Tableau, where the cards above the significator can show what is beyond their control, this card in that position would indicate the person was being driven by needs not fully known to themselves. If it were found below the significator, it would perhaps indicate a person in touch with their deeper emotions and currents.

If the sitter asks about the likely success of a business trip, the Ship card would indicate travel and speculation, perhaps the Whip would signify "work in service," and then the Fish "resources, money, and good fortune." All in all, these cards would be indicative of a successful business trip.

35. The Anchor

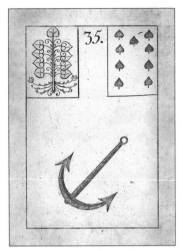

Figure 35. The Anchor

The Anchor is the key symbol of the Game of Hope; it is *the* card of hope. In the game, landing on it was the aim, rather than overshooting, which would mean landing upon the Cross.

In the German tradition, this card is the symbol of work in the sense of one's vocational career—the anchor to life, something that provides stability in a storm yet can also keep you in one place. The card is thus, as are all cards in the Lenormand, modified by the card next to it and surrounding it. The Anchor is a fixed point in a reading, whereas the Ways is the freedom of choice. Where these two cards are in relationship to each other and the sitter's significator card can tell us a lot about their ability to make choices in their current situation. The cards around the Anchor and Ways can also tell us what influences their decisions.

In a literal interpretation, this card can be the significator of career and chosen employment, whether it be through working for a company (Tower or Bear) or for oneself (Fox).

The Anchor is a stabilising influence that takes into account the conditions at play. It is urging caution, especially if the Ship and the Clouds' uncertainty and change are close by. It may be a time to reassess the situation that you are concerned about before venturing into uncharted waters! If this combination was followed by the Sun, it could indicate a waiting period of up to a year, but this could also imply that there will be positive growth with the Sun's presence when the time is right.

36. The Cross

In the Christian backdrop of the original Game of Hope, written into the rules of the game is the notion of the Cross as suffering and adversity. It is more the cross of the gravestone than the cross of sacrifice. It is symbolic of finality without redemption, rather than the more positive reconceptualisation as faith. The Cross, then, is read as

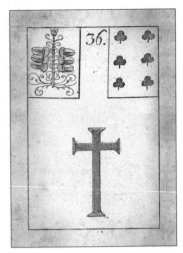

Figure 36. The Cross

struggle, perhaps asking us to maintain faith in the advent of difficult times. It is very much about getting down to the crux of the matter, and is also a card of restriction, fastening us to one place, person, or situation. When combined with the Anchor it may denote a long-term burden.

It denotes the issue burdening us, weighing us down. It could be something on our mind, something we need put down. It is also a card that—as the Stations of the Cross—indicates a whole string of obstacles, one after another; more so than the Mountain, which is one big obstacle, causing us to seek a diversion. If the Cross is combined with the Mice, it is a series of small setbacks causing cumulative trouble.

The Ways is also of importance to this card's meaning when combined together, especially when taking into account the crosslike appearance of the signpost on some illustrations of the Ways, particularly in The Original Lenormand. The Ways alleviates the Cross somewhat, providing some option of movement. If the Cross indicates staying true to faith through burdens, the Ways will keep you true to your path.

Negative, Neutral, and Positive Cards

Certain cards in the Lenormand have a definite positive or negative (favourable or unfavourable) connotation. There is no layering of "this is not a problem, it is an opportunity" language into the literal Lenormand. A snake is an evil and poisonous creature, a mouse will eat you out of house and home. We will list here the various cards in these groups:

- **Neutral Cards:** 1, 17, 19, 22, 25, 27, 28, 29

- **Positive Cards:** 2, 3, 4, 9, 13, 16, 18, 20, 24, 30, 31, 32, 33, 34, 35

- **Negative Cards:** 5, 6, 7, 8, 10, 11, 12, 14, 15 (in some traditions this is a very negative card), 21, 23, 26 (generally), 36

Whilst these associations may be tempered somewhat by the overall context of the cards, as we will see in the following chapter, to stay close to authentic use, they should be treated in the style of definitely good, bad, and indifferent. These groupings may be used to denote if a single or few card layout is generally answering a positive or negative outcome to a straight fortunetelling reading.

We will next start to put these cards together in context, when they really start to speak.

TWO

Reading the Cards in Context

The Lenormand cards are taken as pieces of an alphabet, and we build them up into words and sentences to generate meaning. It is important to learn the cards as a separate language. In this chapter we will take a look at the basics of the Lenormand language to see how cards are modified by the cards near to them and their location in a layout. This approach to reading in context and combination may have been inspired by tea leaf or coffee grounds reading, and those in turn through far more ancient meanings ascribed to objects for divinatory purposes, including dream interpretation and oracular utterances.

Some of these exercises and methods of reading the cards are not used by every reader, so you should try out as many of them as possible to see what really works for you to unlock the cards' meanings. You may find you have a particular skill or understanding in one of these areas, just as you might in learning a foreign language.

Order of Reading

There are three ways in which you can read Lenormand cards when laying them out in a row of two or more cards. They are:

- Blended/Merged

- Linear/Left to Right

- Affected by Following/Right to Left

If we take a simple two-card example of the Clover and the Fish, we can see how these orders take effect. The most important thing is to choose which method works best for you in different circumstances.

Figure 37. The Clover and the Fish

If we blend these two cards together, we generate a lucky fish, perhaps a talisman of good luck. There is a lucky event of some description with regard to our finances and resources, our general material well-being.

If, however, we read these cards in a linear left-to-right sequence like a storyboard, we would say, "First the Clover, then the Fish." That is to suggest that we will have some lucky event that will bring more material benefits thereafter, good resources or work. The lucky event itself—the clover—may have nothing to do directly with what follows; it could even be something like a marriage, which brings financial reward in its own way!

When instead reading from right to left, in effect, we consider that the first card is the object (and this is usually, as it is the nearest card to our significator, or the significator itself, in reading lines in a Grand Tableau) and the following cards each have a roll-back effect on the cards preceding them.

In the simple case of the Clover and the Fish, it is the lucky event that is the object, and the Fish (resources) is applying to it. That might indicate more precisely that the nature of the lucky event will be one of resources—a winning lottery ticket, the finding of a lost wallet that brings reward, and so on.

When this applies to longer sequences, each card modifies the card before it, so the final card in a row is the most influential; it really tells us the most likely outcome and the general deciding factor. A long sequence of generally negative cards that ends in the Star may indicate that our hopes will ultimately be realised through struggle, whilst a sequence of generally positive cards culminating in the Mountain would suggest that we will face obstacles throughout the situation with little absolute result—just another obstacle.

Negative and Positive Cards

Whilst every card in Lenormand is influenced by its position and context, unlike tarot where most cards are given a positive aspect (e.g., the Tower is not just disruption, it is clearing the air to see new horizons), some cards in Lenormand are generally negative, such as the Snake.

There are other cards that might be considered more neutral, such as the Clouds, which are affected by their facing. These cards also show a lack of clarity or confusion, which is neither good nor bad, although it again depends on the surrounding cards.

EXERCISE: NEAR AND FAR

First, we're going to play a game of "near and far," or "hot and cold." This will make sense as we approach the Grand Tableau method later and instill a good habit in reading Lenormand, where combination and context is so very important to interpretation.

It is a simple game based on Japanese grammar, where the distance of an object changes the very word you use to speak about it. We think this is unique to Japanese, and it is very useful to learning the language of the Lenormand.

Imagine a bear. You are looking at it on a screen or from a considerable distance, separated by something. What comes to mind? The bear's movements, perhaps the way it shambles? Make a note in the table below the words that come to mind, "shambling" or "strolling."

Now imagine the bear in the room with you, or very close up! What comes to mind? Other than "Run!"? Perhaps "strength," "power," or "fear." Write that in the other box below.

Then you can repeat the exercise with the following selection of cards:

OBJECT	FAR	NEAR
BEAR	Slow movement, strolling	Roar, power, fear
TREE		
MOON		
GARDEN		
MOUNTAINS		
HEART		
GENTLEMAN		

If you are journaling your discovery of the Lenormand cards, you can of course do this with all the cards to discover your own interpretation of objects near and far to you. It can also be instructive to go back over your keywords and kaleidoscope words and plug them into the near/far table to consider how, for example, the Mice (choosing a keyword such as "disruption") would work under your nose and at a distance. After a while, you can practice near and far with combinations, such as for a question about a sales job. Mice and Bouquet near to you might signify self-doubt if the cards were close at hand (Mice as worrying, Bouquet as self-appreciation in this case), or someone giving you false leads if the two cards were at a distance (an apparent gift like flowers, but something that actually gnaws away at your foundations, the mice).

We will now introduce you to the relative significance of cards depending on their position in what is called the Grand Tableau. The word *tableau* means both "table" and "picture," so it is a wonderful word for our grand spread.

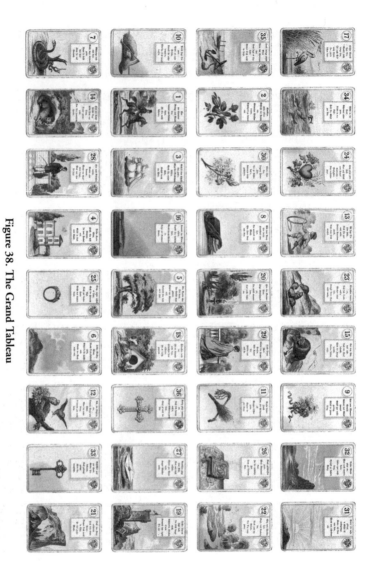

Figure 38. The Grand Tableau

74

Figure 39. Grand Tableaux 9 x 4

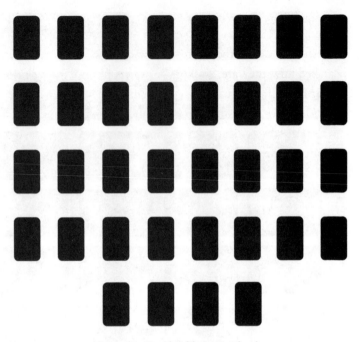

Figure 40. Grand Tableaux 8 x 4 + 4

Cherchez la Femme

The clichéd phrase "cherchez la femme" actually first appears in a novel by Alexandre Dumas set in Paris whose crime inspector regularly uses the phrase, as often the key to any investigation is a woman! So it is fitting we start to investigate our tableaux and relationships by playing a little "search for the woman." In Lenormand, the sitter is represented by either of two cards, the Gentleman or the Lady, as befits their stated gender. We will see later how we can charge the cards and ask the Lenormand questions for a specific purpose, situation, or issue, using key cards such as the Bear for questions of health, for example. For now, we will start with the Gentleman and the Lady.

In most decks, these cards face particular directions, so we can see how they are "looking forward" or "leaving behind" other cards, for a start. How cool is that?

One way of reading is to presume that what is to the left of the sitter's significator (Gentleman or Lady) is the past, and what is to the right is the future.

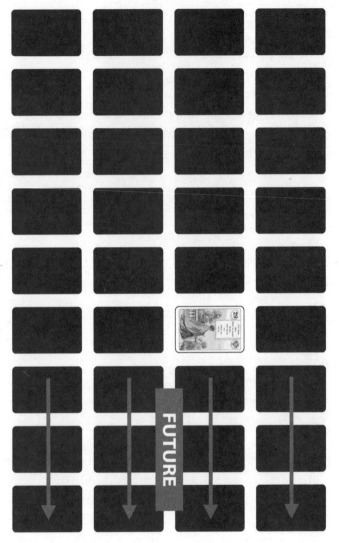

Figure 41. Determining Past and Future

Reading Cards in Any Context

Generally speaking, questions will always focus on one particular area, be it someone's relationship, career, finances, health, travel, lifestyle, and occasionally education and legal issues. In this section we will show how two selected cards can be taken in each of these areas, by themselves or in combination with a number of other cards in sequence.

The Rider in the Context of Work

The Rider card is symbolic of the delivery of communication in many forms, either through the physical delivery of news via the postman or verbal communications in day to day conversation. It can signify the delivery of gossip, where we are reminded of the old saying "don't shoot the messenger."

This card is the effective relaying of communication across various networks. It can also be the phone call you receive, the email, or the text message. News good or bad is delivered a lot swifter these days than via the old-style horseback messenger.

The appearance of this card in the context of work puts a great emphasis on effective communications, making sure the person who needs to get the message gets it loud and clear. The person who needs to get the message could be the one in the office who never listens to what you say. So the Rider can stress the importance of delivering your ideas with clarity.

The meaning of the card of course changes by the influence it takes on from those cards around it. The Rider with the Whip may say "news is troubling," which could be news about unpaid overtime or a form of servitude; you may feel you are being taken advantage of at work. The Whip can be about trouble and strife in your life.

Switched Sequence
- Whip + Rider may say "trouble delivering news." It also may imply trouble getting something across, itself causing strife in a work environment.

Rider in the Context of Finances
- Rider + Whip + Fish = News is troubling regarding money

Switched Sequence
- Fish + Whip + Rider = Money trouble news

Rider in the Context of Health
- Rider + Whip + Coffin = News of troubling illness

Switched Sequence
- Coffin + Whip + Rider = Illness that is troubling news on the way

Rider in the Context of Relationships
- Rider + Tree = News of family

Switched Sequence
- Tree + Rider = Family news to come

- Rider + Heart + Gentleman or Lady + Clover
  = News of love from Gentleman or Lady will
  bring luck (well-being)

Switched Sequence
- Clover + Lady or Gentleman + Heart +
  Rider = Luck (well-being) at finding Lady or
  Gentleman for love and possible marriage as
  dating agency delivers match.

- Rider + Whip + Heart + Mice = Gossip
  delivered (news) brings strife, gnawing
  away at you.

Switched Sequence
- Mice + Heart + Whip + Rider = Gnawing
  feeling that strife will result from gossip in
  future (news)

Rider in the Context of Travel and Lifestyle
- Rider + Ship = Postman delivers travel tickets

Switched Sequence
- Ship + Rider = Holiday travel tickets on
  their way

The Fox in the Context of Work

As mentioned earlier, the Fox is the (somewhat opportunistic) entrepreneur of the Lenormand deck. Remember, however, that this card is not all bad—if you put the Fox with Clover, for example, it could say you will have innovative ideas that make you lucky. As with most divination, there is no "good" or "bad," it's all in how we read it.

- Fox + Garden = Crafty behaviour expected at a conference

Switched Sequence

- Garden + Fox = An innovative conference

Three Cards with the Fox

- Fox + Garden + Tower = Crafty behaviour during a conference—watch out for yourself

Switched Sequence

- Tower + Garden + Fox = Be on watch at the conference for crafty behaviour/sly tricks

Below we have added Clover to the sequence, which modifies the meaning, putting a more positive slant on the interpretation. Every Lenormand cloud has a silver lining, which is why it is so important to read cards in combination. Otherwise it's akin to tearing the last page out of a novel and never having the full story.

Four Cards with the Fox

- Fox + Garden + Tower + Clover = Watching out at the conference for crafty behaviour/sly tricks could prove advantageous.

Having introduced ourselves to these sequences and combinations, as well as the general layout of the Grand Tableau, we will now move on to the GT itself. You may feel you *need* a G & T to tackle it, however, we are now reasonably prepared!

THREE

The Grand Tableau

We will now introduce the *Grand Tableau*, which you may be surprised to find that you now know how to read using the skills we covered in our previous chapters. Though it will take practice, you have the essentials already in your head, so let's apply them.

The Grand Tableau

There are many ways to read Lenormand cards; however, unlike tarot they rarely depend on a fixed positional meaning. That is to say, there are not (yet) whole books of spreads where, for example, the card in position 3 indicates the sitter's hopes or the card in position 9 represents how others see them.

Lenormand cards are read usually in lines (linear Lenormand), curves (horseshoes), circles, or in tableau, usually laid out in a block. We are going to start in the deep end and look at the tableau; it is the best way to teach the cards in relationship to their relative positions.

So, let's scare ourselves *un petit peu* first by seeing what we will end up being able to read when we have finished. Take a deep breath, and ...

Now, whilst that may seem a little scary—all thirty-six cards laid out with not a positional meaning to read—that's only because most of us are tarot readers or entirely new to cartomancy.

Before we go ahead and learn some practices so we can develop our skills, and then return to apply them to this method, just a few words about the Tableau.

There are several ways of laying this out. The two most widely used are the 9 x 4 (nine columns in four rows) or the 8 x 4 + 4 (eight columns in four rows with a fourth row of four cards below). We will use the 9 x 4 for this lesson and return to the other method later, as at present we are only interested in relative positions. We hope you did your "near and far" exercise earlier, as it will help you now.

We will now introduce the Grand Tableau, which you may be surprised to find that you now know how to read using the skills we have covered in our previous chapters. Though it will take practice, you have the essentials already in your head, so let's apply them.

Simpler Layouts
Leading to the Grand Tableau

We have seen that the Grand Tableau can be laid out in at least two or three different manners, so we will continue to keep things simple with the 9 x 4 layout. However, before we start, we will look at some simpler layouts, starting with the 3 x 1 three-card layout.

We also need to introduce the idea of "charged cards"— that is, cards that act as compass points, about which we navigate and find our bearings. These are somewhat similar to the significator in a tarot spread, but they're different enough to require explanation.

A charged card is taken out of the deck by choice to relate to the question being asked. In general cases, this is the Gentleman card for a male sitter and the Lady card for a female sitter. In other specific instances, the card is chosen according to one's correspondences and keywords. Here are some cards for you to consider.

Charged Cards (Key Cards)

Relationship	The Heart
Health	The Bear
Spiritual Life	The Coffin (sometimes used for immediate health issues)
Career	The Fox
Home/Domestic	The House
Education	The Book
Contracts	The Ring
Relocation/Travel	The Ship

The appropriate card is first taken out of the deck and "charged" (in rune work we would call this "loading") by concentrating on the card. There are various other actions one can take to charge the card, but they aren't covered here and a moment of concentration will suffice.

The card is then replaced in the deck so we know what we are looking for when it is laid out with other cards in any form of layout. It provides a beacon for us to use in highlighting the tableau. Consider it a lighthouse, shining brightly on the cards around it (but perhaps missing those right next to it) and less brightly on the cards far away from it.

If we are performing a quick three-card spread, we simply shuffle and go through the deck face-up until we find the charged card. We select the card above it and below it, and lay these out together for our reading.

In any case of shuffling, you may wish the sitter to shuffle, or you may shuffle and allow the sitter to then split the deck into three piles (with their left hand) and then restack them into one deck.

Three-Card Reading (Career)

Let us imagine our sitter has asked about his or her career. We are to perform a three-card spread. We charge the **Fox** card, and then shuffle (or allow the sitter to shuffle) and perform a three-deck split. When the cards are placed back in a single pile, we turn them face-up and work through them carefully to locate the charged Fox card.

The card immediately above it, we place down on the table, then the Fox itself, then the card immediately below it. Of course, you can select two cards above and below for a five-card layout; three cards above and below for a seven-card layout; and so on.

Figure 42. Three-Card Career Reading

In this example, the Letter is to the left and the Child to the right of the Fox. Using our essence keywords, we see this as "an innocent sentiment." As a sentiment is a combination of beliefs and emotions, we read this as being completely guileless with regard to career (the young child.) Unless this sitter is looking for employment in childcare or other related fields (for example, entertainment) this does not bode well for job-hunting.

The Letter itself may be read literally that the person will receive an offer but going into it wide-eyed is ill-advised, as otherwise they will be eaten. (The fox has caught the bird in the central image.) This is very much a warning.

Nine-Card Reading (Romance)

In this next reading, we look at a charged card for relationships, the Heart. Whilst generally we would look mainly at the placement and relationships between the Gentleman and the Lady cards for matters of romance, we can also look at the Heart card to see the sitter's emotional state within the situation.

In this nine-card reading we have placed the heart at the centre of the cards for the purpose of teaching—this will make sense later in this lesson. For now, just work with us *un moment* and examine this layout.

Take a look at these cards in relationship to each other. One thing that immediately strikes us is that bearing down on the emotional state of the Heart (reading right to left) are the top three cards, together showing "a proposal of faithful reliability." The sitter's highest expectation of relationship is to be given a long-lasting statement of trust. When we look at the three cards below, we might see that they have reached a standstill in their self-appreciation (Anchor + Bouquet + Coffin), the Coffin doubly signifying a recent change of state (perhaps a divorce or other breakup) and also their self-initiation and image. With the Bouquet "appreciation" is turned into a self-image and self-worth state, rather than someone else's appreciation.

We hope you can see how we must read the cards **together** first, in batches, sets, montages, vignettes, scenarios, scenes, and tableaux. It makes it much easier.

Now, what about the **Ways** and the **Stork** either side of the heart? Is there something promising in the sitter's emotional life?

Figure 43. Heart (Emotional) Nine-Card Layout

92

Nine-Card Reading (Travel)

Let's do another nine-card reading, this time for a question about travel. A sitter has come to ask us about their prospects for travel: should they look to travel or settle down?

Travel relates to the Ship, so after charging that card, we could first place it on the table and shuffle. Then we'll cut and draw eight cards to surround it. We could alternatively shuffle, find the Ship, place it on the table, and surround it with the next eight cards in the deck. There's another method you'll learn at the end of this lesson, but for now, let's look at this next layout together.

Let us also add that our sitter in this case is a young man, so we can immediately see that the Gentleman card with the Clouds ahead of him shows change and transition. Whilst he will likely seek stability (the Tree) on the other side of that rapid change, he will be forced to travel anyway, as the Ship is above him.

How about we use our keyword kaleidoscope to see what the Snake might mean here?

We take a look at Snake + Ship + Clouds as they corner the Gentleman. That's:

- Stealth + Adventure + Transition
- Stealth + Adventure = Spying
- Adventure + Transition = Exploration
- Stealth + Transition = Disguise

We can collapse our kaleidoscope into one word: Spying + Exploration + Disguise = Safari. It certainly looks like the cards are suggesting a high-octane adventure-type trip where the sitter will have to dress up for the climate or culture.

Now do the same for the Scythe, Sun, and Messenger in the top-right corner. They are further away from the Gentleman but influence somewhat his activities with regard to travel, being on the shadow side to him (the Ship).

Figure 44. Ship (Travel) Nine-Card Layout

Nine-Card Reading (Education)

Let's take what we have learnt and practiced in these nine-card methods and now apply it to a sitter who has come to us to ask a question about education. The sitter wishes to leave her current job, but is unsure how to go about retraining or learning, whether she should invest, do it full-time or part-time, or stick with her current career. Whilst this is related to career, it is more about education and upgrading skills so we'll charge the Book card.

In this case, let us first imagine a cross of vertical and horizontal lines; take a reading as to what is directly influencing the sitter's perspective on her education. Next, we'll look at the diagonal cards to discover any possible routes.

We cover this more later in our chapter on diagonals, but for now, let us use it as a way of applying our skill in two separate examples.

So here we can read the Stork and the Tower either side of the Book indicating a "delivery of vision"—almost like receiving a clear plan of the future. This shows that the sitter already has all the information required to make the decision, like a syllabus of life.

The Letter and the Lily top and bottom together show a "pure invitation," an offer that will be absolutely what the sitter requires.

We have not done anything here other than put together our essence keywords from the earlier chapter, but now we can work on our interpretation, perhaps by placing these phrases together to read "you will receive an offer that will meet your vision, and you are advised here to commit yourself to it absolutely cleanly, separating it out from all other concerns. It must remain yours and be done for your own self-worth, not for others."

Let's now clarify this insight with the diagonals.

The **Fox** and **Coffin** seem to be the most "negative" images here, however, they are not so when taken *en masse*; the cunning of the **Fox** with the Book shows rapid learning to good effect and the **Coffin** shows a transition or new state of affairs that will arise from the new education. Again, it is suggested the sitter quit her current job and make space for the course alone.

Similarly, the Ring and the Lady here show that the proposal will be pleasing and emotionally satisfying.

Figure 45. Book (Education) Nine-Card Layout

Figure 46. Book Layout Cross Cards

Figure 47. Book Layout Diagonal Cards

Now let's take a final look at further layouts of 3 x 3 for two other perennial topics, health and spirituality.

In these two cases, we will give you a couple of pointers, ask you to look at the readings, and apply your skills and practice to interpret the layouts.

Nine-Card Reading (Health)
Exercise: Bear Reading

- What will be good for the sitter's health, according to this layout?

- What tends to draw the sitter to practices that are bad for their health?

- What is the importance of the Mice + Birds + Scythe?

- Look at the images of the Bear + Broom. What does this say about willpower?

Exercise: Coffin Reading

- What might flowers of all kinds signify to the spiritual life?

- What is the difference between a house and a garden? What could that mean?

- Compare the two columns, left and right. What might these suggest?

Figure 48. Bear (Health) Nine-Card Layout

Figure 49. Coffin (Spiritual Life) Nine-Card Layout

The Grand Tableau

We have seen how we can derive so much meaning from 3 x 3 card layouts, and you may be wondering when you will build up to the incredible 4 x 9 thirty-six-card Grand Tableau. Well, *mesdames et messieurs*, we have a surprise for you—you have already learned the Grand Tableau! *C'est vrai!*

It is indeed true. Take another look at all those 3 x 3 layouts you have been reading, and then take a look at the following single Grand Tableau.

That's right! Every single reading you have done in this chapter—whether it be three cards for the career of the sitter, nine cards for health or spiritual purpose, relocation concerns or their romantic life—*they are all from the same single Grand Tableau.* This is the incredible scope of learning Lenormand; one singular layout can be used to read the entire range of concerns and issues any sitter may present.

You don't have to keep laying out different cards or spreads as you might in a tarot reading; the method is actually a lot simpler than shuffling and searching for charged cards, counting piles, or anything—just lay out all the cards and read the tableau. In between each significator card being read for health, wealth, or love, we reset our meanings for the other cards. In other words, the Fox can now mean something entirely different in the next part of the reading. The way meanings may change is one of the most fundamental differences in practice to tarot. It also makes for a reading that can last two hours at least, so it is best to take time into consideration if you are interested in adding the GT to a professional practice.

Figure 50. The Grand Tableau Master

105

Exercise: Near and Far

If you have completed the previous exercises, you may consider how the various 3 x 3 layouts relate to each other—where they overlap (and how you read the same cards differently in each case!)—and where they are far apart. Which charged cards are near and far to each other, and how might that add another layer to your reading? Which cards that caused concern in one part of the tableau also cause concern in another?

It may take a while to realise just how powerful a method this is, and how you can now profoundly apply the essential skills you have already learnt to interpreting a full tableau. In our next chapter, we will deepen our reading with an introduction of the houses of Lenormand, although it is suggested you practice for a while without using the houses.

We also recommend you continue to practice with full tableaux, even if you only read part of them. Do not get into a habit of laying out only a few cards; this sort of laziness leads your brain down a more limited avenue.

FOUR

Zones and Shadows

In this lesson we will consider the whole Grand Tableau and a few smaller areas for your practice. We will look at our own personal and contemporary methods of considering the whole GT with zones, making use of correspondences from other systems. Whilst we only cover the basics here, there are many more templates that can be usefully applied to the GT to provide a reading's clarification, correlation, and confirmation.

The Zones

We can consider the GT a scenario that reflects upon all aspects of our sitter's field, form, and fate (see the book of that same name, *Field, Form and Fate* by Michael Conforti). When seen as a field, we can divide it into different zones. Whilst some zones are dependent on how the cards fall, others can be seen in the fixed matrix of the GT. When we layer the two, we get a very comprehensive and flexible way of reading Lenormand.

In these illustrations, we will use the 8 x 4 + 4 layout so we can learn to use this variation by considering the bottom four cards as a new set called *label cards*.

In this illustration, we see the cards around the edge of the GT are considered the frame. These are often useful to be read together midway through the reading in order to give some overall context and summary. We can break this frame down into distinct components.

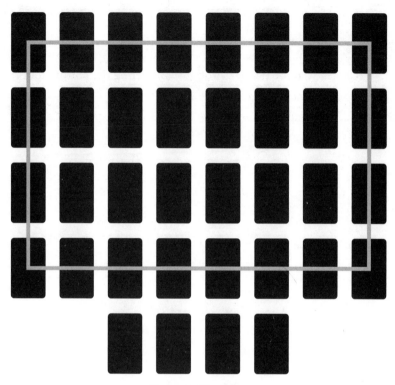

Figure 51. The Frame

Past and Future Frame

Read the column to the left as a past frame and the column to the right as a future frame, irrespective of the deck or other elements of the reading.

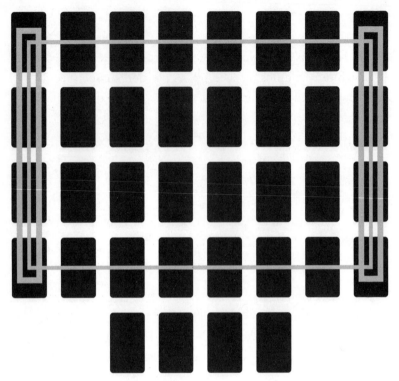

Figure 52. Past Frame and Future Frame

The four cards in the left column give us an indication of the past of the current situation, or effectively what sitters always return to when considering their life, old visions, patterns, habits, strongest memories, etc. This column shows us what has made them who they are in the present as well as what may need uncovering or even redeeming to make substantial changes in the present scenario.

The four cards in the right column give us an indication of the future—where sitters can see from where they are right now. This may be limiting or stretching them, depending on the other cards and contexts we have already read in the GT.

Note that these two columns are sort of different from the past/future columns dictated by the position and perspective of the charged card, e.g., the Gentleman. Where the card falls in a male sitter's reading may indicate that most of the GT to the right is the future. If his card has fallen in the left column and he faces right, it means that he's stuck in the patterns of his past.

As the epigraph of this chapter illustrates, the aim of our reading should be to promote self-governance; the use of these frames in combination with our previous lessons gives a powerful mechanism for layering a GT reading.

Zones of the Spiritual and Mundane Life

You can consider the top and bottom rows as the spiritual frame (highest aspirations) and material frame (manifestation, practicalities), which is useful in some questions, particularly when pairing.

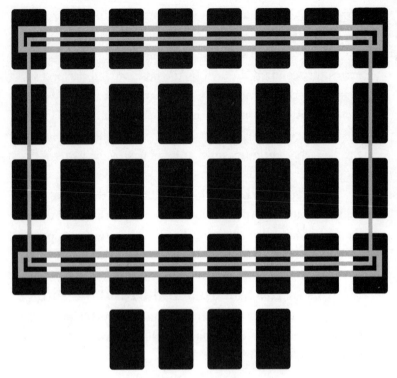

Figure 53. Upper and Lower Frame

As with the past/future columns, you can pair/compare cards to drill down into the detail of the overall reading without losing the gestalt of the whole.

Here is an example of a reading we did where we have taken out just the top row and bottom row of our GT and read them as two rows, then paired.

Figure 54. Example of Above and Below Frame

- The Above Cards: 1, 31, 34, 36, 23, 30, 2, 20

The above cards speak of a spiritual life motivated by the giving of communications; this is evident with card number 1, the Rider. This is powered by the energy of the Sun, so the willpower to carry on is there, and the resources will be provided with the presence of the Fish card so long as the intent is true.

The Cross represents a certain burden that accompanies the journey, yet reassures. The work is done quietly and steadily, prolific and slow in nature, in the spirit of the Mice card. The Lily warns against neglecting one's inner life, and it cautions against thinking the goal has been reached—things have only just begun. It would be better to maintain a life of simple discipline than to aim too high and be left wanting.

This lifetime is about showing the best of what one is, rather than being superficial. As Shakespeare wrote, "lilies that fester smell far worse than weeds." The focus is on not putting off one's duties. The **Clover** is about "knowing thyself"—personal identity, with the Lily also indicating an inner purity that must be preserved even if taken into the garden of external life.

The Garden is the "social self," which must be presented in integrity with the "inner self" of the Lily. The Garden must not be a place where one is seduced into behaving in an inauthentic manner.

- The Below Cards: 5, 32, 22, 9, 15, 27, 16, 4

In day-to-day life, these cards show, particularly with the Tree and the House bordering either end of this row, the importance of keeping one's resources close to hand. If used wisely, the Tree can provide a self-sustaining resource and shelter—but it can also be wasted and turned into planks which then rot. The Moon casts a light on the sitter's practical life, showing a need to connect to intuition along the Ways card— that inner voice should be listened to, and the sitter should find the Bear's strength in the ability to communicate (the Letter). The Star shows that the sitter's day-to-day life must be steady and not at risk of burnout; the sitter should favor long-term planning and avoid crash-and-burn syndrome.

When we look at the pairs of Above and Below, we can delve into the sitter's most profound spiritual life issues, how it relates to their practical life, and vice versa. I provide a brief note here of what might be explored; you can see that this is a session in itself.

- 1 + 5: Messenger and Tree—the importance

of channelling ancestral knowledge and learning from one's own deep history.

- 31 + 32: Sun and Moon—the balance of will and emotive decision-making.

- 34 + 22: Fish and Ways—the sitter's spiritual resources can be nourished by observing signs and acting upon them. Even if the sitter asked, "How should I act?" we can answer this by looking in the original GT at the cards above the Ways card, we could look at the house in which it had fallen, etc. This is the power of L-space: it provides what our first quote of this chapter called a "panorama".

- 36 + 4: Cross and Bouquet—applying appreciation to one's spiritual life with outside observation and practice, showing reverence.

- 23 + 15: Mice and Bear—from humility can be drawn strength.

- 30 + 6: Lily and Letter—putting things off will cause festering within.

- 2 + 7: Clover and Star—returning to one's own original dreams and visions will bring good fortune.

- 20 + 4: Garden and House—finding the balance of inner and outer life.

We hope yet again you will see that even whilst these pairs provide us acres of information to relate to the sitter, we would be best served by seeing them in the full GT and expanding outwards from each pair. In providing these zones, the aim is to give you lots of diving boards into the full ocean.

The Four Pin Cards

We can then look at what we call the **pin cards.** These are the four cards that would pin the GT up if it were hung on a wall, and show a sibyl how the sitter is holding him- or herself in a life situation. These four cards are the sitter's unique signature or strategy for dealing with the stresses (and tranquilities) of his or her life.

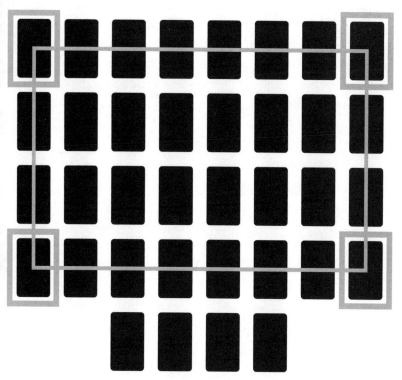

Figure 55. The Four Pin Cards

The Label Cards

Finally, we can also look at those lower four cards in the 4 x 8 + 4 version of the GT, which we call the label cards. If we imagine the GT as a picture, a *tableau vivant*, then the four cards at the bottom are the label. They give the essential details or characteristics of the image. In cartomantic tradition, these are the "verdict."

The label cards tell us, in no particular order:

- The **history** of the scenario (Is it in its early stages? Middle? Late or declining?)

- The overall **style** of the scenario, that is to say, is it a formal or informal situation? Is it a matter of the heart or the mind?

- The **subject** matter—what is really being communicated?

- The **uniqueness** at play for this particular sitter. What sets this scene apart from other depictions of the same?

As an example, if we had the following four cards in the label area:

Figure 56. Label Cards

This would tell us the following about the sitter's life:

- History: Heritage, long-standing
- Style: Traditional, following a pattern

- Subject: Creating a space by making decisions—finding your place

- Uniqueness: Being thrust into what the sitter is supposed to be doing and following through.

We would suspect that the sitter had been employed or in a relationship for a long time, and had now been thrust into a totally new situation. Whilst for many it is a common subject to "find one's place,", this sitter has a unique position (the in medias res aspect), and any immediate decisions will set the course for some time to come.

You can assign four fixed positional meanings to these four label cards, but we find that closes off the elegance, grace, and profound power of L-space to easily express complex situations.

The Hidden Cross

A more advanced template you can consider is the "hidden cross," comprising the following cards.

The four cards in the centre of the GT give the hidden cross its pivot point and can be taken as the "hub" or "crux" of the matter, particularly in the sitter's daily or mundane world. Since these four cards are the "hub" of the matter, sometimes I take a peek at these first before I start navigating the whole GT in order to get my bearings, then I go look at the charged card and read on.

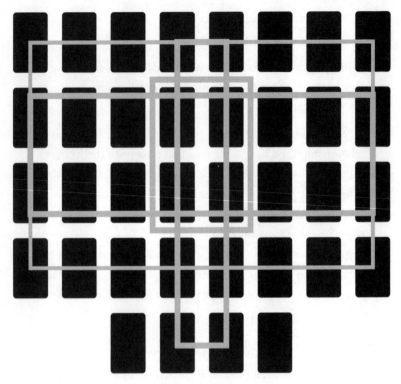

Figure 57. The Hidden Cross

Reading Whole or Linear

In all these templates, the cards are read as we have learnt—**together.** They have no unique positional meaning; they are always arising as a whole scenario. If you lay them out as a block or a row, you can decide if you wish to read them left to right, or right to left, in a linear fashion.

If you do, you need to decide in advance which card impacts on the other. Does the first card apply to the second you read, or vice versa?

As an example, in a linear reading, you might have the first two cards of the Key and the Coffin.

Figure 58. The Key and the Coffin

We might consider it like this: is the Key in the Coffin, or on the outside? It might really make a difference! This is where most of the books remain somewhat unclear—when they provide pairings (many do), they maintain the same interpretation no matter the relative position of the two cards. This is fine in a holistic-type reading where all the cards are seen together and as a whole, but it is problematic—well, confusing (mainly to T-space readers)—when reading in a linear fashion. Unsurprisingly, everyone asks, particularly those travelling from T-Space to L-Space.

If we read the Key then the Coffin, according to Treppner, we get a simple interpretation: "It will get better soon." However, if we read the Coffin *then* the Key, we get much the same, but with a proviso, "It will get better soon, [however] there will be a minor misfortune affecting your security, but nothing dramatic." That is to say, the Key (locked) will be breached by the Coffin's impact.

Generally, a good rule is to say the second card applies to or modifies the reading of the first. In this case, "security" **first** from the key, *then* the "change" implied by the Coffin. If we were to read them the other way around, it would be the change of the Coffin being locked down by the Key—quite the opposite interpretation.

As usual, find what works best for you, and once you have decided on a method, stick to it, review it often, and gradually develop your own methodology. We are all unique oracles.

Shadowing

Shadowing is a slightly quirky element I (Tali) have added to my own readings over time, as I believe that when a card is very close to another, it is sometimes not so obviously reading as "strong influence" but rather "too close to see."

As a result, I often read the cards immediately surrounding a card as "shadowing" it. This might be compared very loosely to tarot reversals; it adds a certain angle to readings that often provokes sudden intuitive insight. You might like to try this and see if it works for you also.

Any card immediately next to another can be seen as shadowing it. The potential readings are endless because you may be looking at several cards shadowing your key card, the Gentleman or Lady, or a few cards shadowing a card which you have knighted and is in a particular house of interest—this is where we cannot really give rules.

The best analogy to this is not chess but the game of Go. With just a few very simple rules and a couple of differently sized boards, the mind cannot really fathom fixed rules like chess. Go offers a graceful and elegant flow of patterns and is played through like the best Lenormand reading.

You might like to read *Go! More Than a Game* by Peter Shotwell for more on the game's mechanics and aesthetics. The science of "pattern recognition"—particularly as it applies to chess and tarot—is something Marcus Katz has written about in *Tarosophy*.

1. The Rider/Messenger:
   Communications/Liaison
   Shadow Words: Noise, chatter, gossip

   An example is the Bear and Anchor shadowed by the Rider. This might indicate internal chatter, doubts and uncertainty, paranoia, and bouts of depression that may affect health and mental/emotional well-being. Another example could be the Mice and Child shadowed by the Rider: the state of being unaware of an impending problem due to misinformation.

2. The Clover: Identity/Luck
   Shadow Words: Bereft/Misfortune

   The Clover can be about identity, in that the clover (shamrock) is considered as the national flower of Ireland, and the symbol is very rooted in national identity there.

   The Stars and Tree cards shadowed by the Clover could indicate weariness, fatigue, and feeling that your life is dull and no longer what you want. A lack of belonging, alienation, a lack of feeling appreciated, losing track of our faith, spiritual identity. This could be a time of midlife crisis and a feeling of regret for what you have not created.

It is interesting to note that if the Clover card is combined with the Mountain card, it can signify the discovery and journeying toward spiritual "identity," the reason for this being that "when clover is located upon a mountain it comes to signify knowledge of the divine 'essence" gained by hard endeavour" (Cirlot).

3. The Ship: Adventure
Shadow Word: Speculation

A reckless energy could be at work. The Snake and Book cards shadowed by the Ship would be a blatant misuse of information for ulterior motives; however the Ship shadowing this would show that the deception is easily discovered. It might show that someone is risking discovery because they have become carried away with their own cleverness.

4. The House: Security
Shadow Word: Possessiveness

The House casts a shadow that, whilst providing cover and sanctuary, also leaves one outside. This cutting-off from resources can lead to possessiveness and neediness through fear of losing security.

The shadow of the House then can bring
caution, introversion, and passiveness,
the proverbial "sticking one's head in the
sand."

The Key and Stork cards shadowed by
the House card indicate misuse of power
due to putting too much emphasis on
gaining wealth. There could be a misuse of
credit cards, spending beyond your means,
in order to keep up with those you deem to
be successful. Not be able to pay back, not
be able to deliver what you have promised!

5. The Tree: Longevity
   Shadow Words: Stubbornness; an act of
   overreaching and straying from the source

   The Tree shadowing the Scythe and Heart
   can mean being too intent on being overly
   disciplined, overly motivated, and not
   enjoying life's pleasures as a result. All that's
   left is exhaustion. Life is also about pacing
   the journey and enjoying the moment. It
   is not merely how quickly you reach the
   destination; take time to enjoy the scenery.
   Is this a lesson the sitter needs to learn?

6. The Clouds: Transition
   Shadow Words:
   Unpredictability, variability

   The warning of those we may describe as

fair-weather friends. Be wary of putting too much faith in those you do not truly know; they may shift their allegiance. Does this ring true? Stormy relationships portended.

If we apply this to the Ship and Fox cards, abandonment is very much suggested here—rats abandon the sinking ship, travel is not advised without planning well beforehand. Beware of shifty behaviour; somebody could let you down. Does something seem too good to be true? Invariably, gut feelings are the correct ones, so you must trust these instincts and act accordingly to make changes.

7. The Snake: Stealth
   Shadow Word: Sabotage
   There are things at work we are hardly aware of; we carry on day to day, perhaps oblivious to the external forces that can wreak havoc. You cannot prepare for every eventuality and just have to accept the inevitable. Or do you?

   The Snake shadowing the Mountain and Anchor implies that a longstanding stubborn situation is not going to go away on its own, insidious problems that have built up over time and have not been addressed are going to come to the fore...

or the warning could be that this could
happen in the future if you do not act now!

8. The Coffin: Initiation
Shadow Word: Tribulation
To step into the unknown brings with it
burden and responsibility.

The Coffin shadowing the Dog and
Child cards shows a test of loyalty, feelings
of being judged by others, losing vigour
and enthusiasm, being kept to heel, and
not being allowed to be footloose and
fancy-free due to responsibilities. Perhaps
there is a feeling that all the fun has
evaporated out of life.

This shadow is about the burden of
codependency and the accompanying pain
attributed to the impending fear of losing
a significant other or desired state. To love
and to be loved back is a blessing and a
curse. A loss of innocence is possible as
well.

Heaven lies about us in our infancy!
Shades of the prison-house begin to close
Upon the growing boy.
—William Wordsworth

9. The Bouquet: Appreciation
Shadow Word: Sycophancy

Casting a shadow over the Lady and Gentleman cards is indicative of a superficial relationship grounded too much in flattery and not in speaking the truth. What is said is done to gain another's favour and affection. A person's motives may be suspect—be wary! Also question the motives if there a whiff of guilt in this emotional equation.

This card shows sycophantic drudgery at work through the use of superficial words and false affections. One can end up forging their own chain of repression. Ulterior motives may be behind a gift.

10. The Scythe: Clearing
Shadow Words: Loss or mourning

This card casting a shadow over the Garden and Lily cards implies that through rash action and curiosity, innocence will be lost that cannot be regained. The indication is painful longing for how things used to be, a state of nostalgia.

I remember, I remember
Where I was used to swing,
And thought the air must rush as fresh
To swallows on the wing;
My spirit flew in feathers then

That is so heavy now.
—Thomas Hood

11. The Rod/Whip: Service
Shadow Word: Drudgery

This card casting a shadow over the
Clouds and Ring talks of commitment to
something or a duty that ends up changing
rapidly from what you originally expected.
You may have entered into a relationship or
work situation thinking you were in charge
of yourself and then find that another
person is calling all the shots—and you are
doing all the running. The outlook could
be dismal if you do not take stock of your
life and act on what you really want.

12. The Birds: Divination
Shadow Word: Receptivity

There is a saying: "Too much knowledge
can be a dangerous thing." The Birds
casting a shadow over the the Moon and
the Cross can suggest an attitude of intense
knowing that lends a false sense of security
in dealing with other peoples' sensitivities
or emotions. Just because you know
something does not mean you should
express it without regard for how it may

affect another person. The indication here can also be the pain and burden that comes with being sensitive and feeling too much.

13. The Child/Little Girl: Ingénue, innocence
Shadow Word: Gullibility

The warning here is of being so naive that the sitter's better nature is being abused.

The Child casting a shadow over the Ways and the Snake could suggest that an ill-considered decision could end up developing into a compromising situation between the sitter and an untrustworthy person. Now is not the time to be so trusting when the sitter does not know the situation or the people very well.

14. The Fox: Cunning
Shadow Word: Malevolence

There is a fine line between ambitious calculation and wishing ill intent on others. It is wise to bear in mind the act of going out and getting what you want merely for selfish ends does not come without repercussion. The Fox card casting a shadow over the Bear and Letter cards speaks of karma and "what goes around comes around." It is never healthy to talk

ill of others; news and gossip may grow out
of control and come boomeranging home!
There is never an action executed without
a return.

15. The Bear: Headstrong
    Shadow Word: Unyielding

    Ever thought about picking a fight with
    a bear? Probably not! Think about the
    Bear casting a shadow over the Tower and
    the Mice; it is about finally seeing what
    has been in plain sight all along, right in
    front of your nose. Perhaps you have been
    behaving like a timid little mouse—now is
    the time to release your inner Bear energy.
    Go on, release your beast, it won't hurt a
    bit!

16. The Star: Creation
    Shadow Word: Proliferation

    There is a school of thought that says we
    are the creator of our own reality; what
    we believe, we become. We therefore have
    to be mindful of what we wish, as one
    negative thought can create another, and
    so on. A restless state of mind grows out
    of control and we are no longer master of
    our reality, spun out of control into a black
    hole.

So if the Star card casts a shadow over the Sun and Moon cards, there could be a bit of rollercoaster ride ahead; maybe your imagination gets the better of you and you become overconfident, plunging yourself into a situation well out of your comfort zone. Bear in mind that this stellar triangulation is pretty powerful; put to good use, the outcome could be used to your benefit, so take heed and be mindful of how you wish upon a star.

17. The Stork: Deliverance
    Shadow Word: Reliance

    This speaks of the danger of becoming too reliant on others for long-term stability— there is a risk attached to the belief that you will be assured security no matter what. You may have surrounded yourself with people you can rely on, a band of supporters who bolster your sense of self-worth. You may expect them to always be there for you when times get tough. In truth, they may not be there for you when you really need them. This in itself can be devestating to your stability.

    The Stork casting a shadow over the Clover and the Ways can indicate insecurity about your identity. You may be aware of where you came from, but what comes next? Questions like "Who am I?", "Where am I going?", "What is my life purpose?", "What's the point of it all?", will be very prominent in the sitter's life. The theme here is a fear of moving forward, potentially losing what one has already.

18. The Dog: Codependency
Shadow Word: Selfishness

Be honest about your true motivation for doing things for others. Are you being pleasant and friendly merely to achieve a certain outcome? Do you want someone else to do a favour for you and are therefore being extra nice? Is someone your friend on your terms, only on your good side when they tell you things you *want* to hear rather than what you *should* hear?

The Dog card shadowing the Key and the Garden indicates a situation where somebody is being kept in the dark. Something is locked away and hidden to avoid a bad reaction, and it is preventing an opportunity to learn and grow via the the outside world and the experiences it holds. The sitter needs to go out, attend events, meet and mix.

19. The Tower: Vision
    Shadow Word: Surveillance

The ability to have vision can bring with it the burden of seeing too much and knowing too much. The shadow this card casts is one of surveillance—we live in times where everything we do is monitored, recorded, and reported. At times it feels as though there's no place to hide from the prying eyes of the Orwellian Big Brother. We are vulnerable to identity theft, cyber-bullying, cyber-stalking, illegal tapping of communications, and endless other invasions of privacy and boundaries.

The Tower card shadowing the Ring and the Fish speaks of jealous, possessive relationships; somebody could be being stalked. The Tower shadow could also indicate that the sitter is consulting the cards too much; they may expect the cards to impart information about someone else to whom they should not be privy. This shadow could be drawing attention to the dangers of obsessive curiosity, in that there are so things that you or another would be better off not knowing. Curiosity killed the cat(fish)!

20. The Garden: Communing
Shadow Word: Social media addiction

There is a so-called condition dubbed social network addiction, coming off the proposed idea that social media is more addictive than cigarettes or alcohol. Facebook, twitter, et al., have become more and more prevalent, must-have, must-do, essential parts of our lives. They expand and enlarge our toolkit of interaction, but also shrink other types of interaction, namely face-to-face, real-life interaction. Maybe we feel we must invest more and more time "feeding the beast" to receive validation of own social worth.

The Garden card shadowing the Birds and Rider cards speaks of Internet bullying, gossip, and an overdependence on social networking for one's sense of self-worth. You need to get back to the basics of socializing: make a phone call, write a letter, go visit somebody in person. Attend an event and make friends in person.

Social networks have changed the ways we interact with each other enormously. One thing that has changed dramatically is the concept of meeting people. This principle was brought to my personal attention a couple of weeks ago when I met a musician for the first time whom I had casually encountered a couple of times online. Oddly enough, neither of us acted as if this were a first meeting.

Users derive a variety of uses and gratifications from social networking sites, including traditional content gratification alongside building social capital, communication, surveillance, and social network enhancement. The different uses and gratifications relate differentially to patterns of usage, with social connection gratifications tending to lead to increased frequency of use, and content gratifications to increased time spent on sites.

21. The Mountain: Durability
    Shadow Word: Toughness

    We all will have at sometime in our lives been accused of being too tough, not having shown enough compassion or understanding when it may have been more appropriate to do so. We may have learnt over the years that those who are too soft get walked all over. The Mountain depicted in the Mountain card has been around a very long time, and it has survived and proved to be durable. The hardships we go through make us tough.

The Mountain card casting a shadow over the Fox card and the Lily can speak of being too calculating and overly forceful, not being flexible and giving way for a change. Remember that spoken of lilies by Shakespeare, in his Sonnet XCIV:

They that have power to hurt, and will do none, That do not do the thing they most do show, Who, moving others, are themselves as stone, Unmoved, cold, and to temptation slow; They rightly do inherit heaven's graces.

And that:

For sweetest things turn sourest by their deeds; Lilies that fester, smell far worse than weeds.

22. The Ways: Choice/decision
    Shadow Word: Responsibility

    The saying "the buck stops here" comes to mind here, meaning that the individual who takes or makes the decision ends up taking full responsibility if all goes wrong at the outcome. We all have to make choices and decisions, and we are aware that along with the process of decision making comes a burden of responsibility. We have to go ahead and bite the bullet.

The Ways card casting a shadow over
the Lady card and the Cross card could
speak of putting too much emphasis on
nurturing and fussing over somebody in
our lives, not allowing them space to make
their own mistakes.

23. The Mice: Productivity
Shadow Word: Dilution

It can be very easy to stretch oneself a
little too far, to push the limit of our
limitations in order to keep up with the
unnecessary want that has become the
norm of our times. We need to slow down
to avoid losing sight of what matters most
and concentrate on quality rather than
quantity. Less is certainly more, especially
if the resource is special. For instance,
compare the quality and unique creation
of limited-edition handmade craftwork
compared to the uniform, mass-produced
products that come off the production line.

The Mice card casting a shadow over
the Letter and Moon brings to mind the
ever-expanding world of social media. We
are in danger of losing the personal touch
of a phone call or personal letter to friends
of old—we no longer have the time. We

exist in a cyberworld that has reshaped
our reality and sacrificed true one-on-one
intimacy.

24. The Heart: Courage
Shadow Words: Foolhardiness/daredevil

There is a propensity to being courageous,
and then there is being foolhardy. Certainly
the former can easily become the latter at
times. You would have to have courage
to walk across Niagara Falls by tightrope,
however many would consider the attempt
foolhardy.

The Heart card casting a shadow over
the Clouds and Anchor would warn against
ignoring warnings to take care and advises
taking action when the safest course and
line of least resistance would be to stay at
home and do nothing at all. Is it that you
think you know it all? Is your behaviour a
bit rash?

25. The Ring: Continuity
Shadow Word: Predictability

When a situation carries on and on
without any change, no end in sight,
this can result in life becoming very
boring. We have such an addiction to
or reliance on routine and habit that we
have almost forgotten what it was like

to be spontaneous. Life becomes very predictable, and we are a prisoner of our own devices. Round and round we go in our vigorous little circle, never moving forward.

Therefore, the Ring card casting a shadow over the Sun and Anchor signifies a stalemate or fixed position; it is a refusal to rest, not allowing the sun to go down, not allowing the anchor to drop. The advice here is to harness the willpower of the Sun and halting power of the Anchor, granting time to plot a new course so change can take place.

26. The Book: Knowledge
Shadow Word: Responsibility

It has been said that a little knowledge is a dangerous thing, such as in the myth of the Pierian Spring at Mount Olympus, a source of knowledge and inspiration, sacred to the Muses. The warning is in reference to how, when we first become familiar with a subject of interest and dip into it, it is like sipping the "shallow draughts" of the Pierian Spring. It can go to our heads and we can easily fool ourselves into believing we know more than we actually do. We all know a know-it-all like that.

The Book casting a shadow over the Rider and the Cross would be very much about someone with a messiah complex. You are advised not to allow yourself to get carried away with your newly found belief or knowledge, resisting the urge to tell everyone about it. There is a need to pull back and take a deep breath. Think deeply but keep these ideas to yourself. Remember that not everyone will appreciate your enthusiasm! So, a little learning *can* be a dangerous thing!

... drink deep, or taste not the Pierian spring: there shallow draughts intoxicate the brain, and drinking largely sobers us again.
—Alexander Pope, "An Essay on Criticism"

27. The Letter: Sentiment
Shadow Word: Regression

Consider old-fashioned letter writing to our nearest and dearest, the care invested in a more pensive approach to communicating our thoughts and feelings. Such letters can be kept and treasured in a sentimental manner, and it would not be quite the same to keep our laptop or iPad under our pillow! However, the downside to letter communications is that in reality, it is time consuming and very slow on all levels.

28. The Gentleman: Analytical
    Shadow Word: Cynical

    Here we have a male figure in your circle who is prone to being a little bit cynical. It is almost guaranteed that if you believe in something truly, he will want to disprove it. There could be an argument waiting in the wings.

    The Gentleman card casting a shadow over the Sun and Anchor could spell out a period of unrest and agitation. If the sitter is asking about a relationship issue, this could mean the sitter is in for a very rocky ride or that they just aren't going anywhere in the relationship; the two energies just feed off each other.

29. The Lady: Intuitive
    Shadow Word: Nervousness

    Just as a little knowledge can be a dangerous thing, as seen in the Book's shadow entry, the ability to tune into the energies around us can also be detrimental. If not kept grounded, this way of being can leave us open to exhaustion. There are times when we need to be able to withdraw, and conserve and consolidate our energy on all levels, emotional and physical. We cannot be all things to all people all the time.

The Lady card casting a shadow over the Fish and the Owl/Birds card brings in a swarm of nervous energy; this combination showing up for the sitter in regard to a home/money/security situation would warn of not responding to the situation with a knee-jerk reaction. The person needs to look at areas in life where general resources and personal energy resources are being drained. The sitter need to ask who in his or her life acts out the role of psychic vampire, and then take necessary actions of self-protection.

30. The Lily: Purity
    Shadow Word: Reservation

    A man who loves with purity considers not the gift of the lover, but the love of the giver.
    —Thomas à Kempis

    This shadow is about holding back and not giving. There is an air of reservation or being reserved when the Lily card casts its shadow over the Heart and Key. If these combinations materialise in the session, the sitter needs to delve deep into their heart and ask what they are holding back from expressing to another in their life, or who is holding back from them.

You give little when you give of your possessions; it is when you give truly of yourself that you truly give. —Kahlil Gibran

31. The Sun: Will
Shadow Word: Obsession

When we get the bit between our teeth and let ourselves get carried away with the buzz of creating, it's hard to take a break. The urge of completion compulsion kicks right in, and you keep on at it until you are satisfied. This state of being ends up being the shadow of the Sun card, casting its shadow of obsession on the Anchor card and Heart card. The situation recalls to mind the movie Groundhog Day, an endless repetition of the same old thing over and over again. In a reading on relationships, well, you can imagine what that implies…Visualise the Anchor and the Heart being one entity, thrown overboard constantly. Just as you settle down, the heart (stability) gets tugged up again. This sort of relationship is in a state of constant flux—something has got to give.

32. The Moon: Dreams
    Shadow Word: Fantasy

    Some dreams are beautiful, and some can turn into nightmares literally overnight. This is especially so if we lose our grasp on reality, which is never good. We may find ourselves trying to live out those fantastical dreams in our daylight hours, and in the stark daylight there is no grounding or reality to them at all.

    The Moon card casting a shadow over the Cross and Clover cautions against taking a gamble or speculation gone too far. The sitter may be fooling themselves that a situation they are embroiled in is going to change for the better. They may need to reassess and think about pulling out.

33. The Key: Access
    Shadow Word: Control

    The Key can be a tool for release, or it can used to lock something away. In certain circumstances this can promote oppression and control. The Key card casting a shadow (control) over the Ship and Whip cards during a sitting speaks of a life not being lived, opportunities being missed.

This could be a career situation where a promotion is not forthcoming, and there is a feeling of not being valued for the hard work and dedication shown. It can also be about a relationship that has become hard work and is not moving forward; there is a feeling of being all washed up.

34. The Fish: Resources
Shadow Word: Need

The Fish card can be all about resources and making the most of your abilities in order to obtain these precious resources. We carry on working to achieve this result. The downside is that we may find ourselves driven by need alone. We may end up compromising what we really want in life to satisfy this need. Thus the shadow of the Fish card is need. If this card casts a shadow over the Book and Rider during a sitting, it could indicate that the sitter is not following a route in life true to their purpose. Perhaps they need to undergo a period of learning or training to fulfil their true purpose in life rather than to keep the proverbial wolf from the door.

35. The Anchor: Standstill
Shadow Words: Burden, obsolescence

The appearance of the Anchor as a symbol in the Lenormand draws attention to an aspect of the sitter's life that needs to become grounded in some way. There has been too much movement in their life, and the Anchor speaks of a need to settle down and stop seeking. In addition to being about a situation, it could also be about a person to whom the sitter is close. The Anchor casting a shadow across the Dog and Fox is about male energy out of control.

36. The Cross: Faith
    Shadow Word: Hope

    The Cross's shadow is about a false sense of reality, wishing on a star, and/or things that may be beyond one's reach. The Cross card casting a shadow upon the House and the Ways suggests that there is an important choice to be made, and a bad decision based on pie-in-the-sky dreams could bring the situation instability. The sitter may need to take a more realistic approach to the situation, and perhaps accept that they may be deceiving themselves.

Conclusion

We hope you will find, with a bit of practice, that the Lenormand is a straight-talking friend for life. However, like any friend it may wait for you to ask the right question, so that it knows that you are ready to listen to its answer. It's always in the question, with these cards, so ask with consideration and remain open to the answer given to you.

To get comfortable quickly with the cards, become familiar with the meanings of the thirty-six images. The beauty and simplicity of Lenormand is that the symbols are easily recognisable even to the absolute beginner to the art of cartomancy.

The Clover Leaf, for example, brings a "little luck"; the Dog we all know as a "loyal friend." The Stork is symbolic of "delivery" or "return." And with just these simple words, using three cards we can read "A little luck with a loyal friend returning."

The Lenormand speaks a universal language, one that is easy to learn. It is an excellent starting point for learning the skills of divination and one that will become a constant companion for any card reader. As a truly historic deck too, you are learning the bare bones of cartomancy when you pick up the Lenormand, giving you a good foundation for other decks such as tarot and oracle cards. If you are an existing reader, you will find that learning the very different language of Lenormand gives you new insight into your other reading methods.

To use this deck, always go back to basics—the literal meaning of the cards. The Bouquet and the House might be read as a "domestic gift," but this combination could simply foretell someone bringing flowers to your house.

Have fun, practice, and keep it simple. This deck of cards, you will soon discover, is indeed like life—a game of hope built from the material of your dreams.

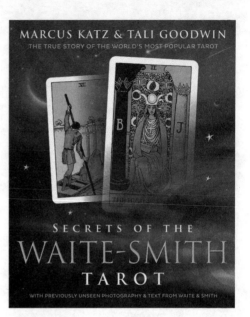

MARCUS KATZ & TALI GOODWIN

THE TRUE STORY OF THE WORLD'S MOST POPULAR TAROT

SECRETS OF THE
WAITE-SMITH
TAROT

WITH PREVIOUSLY UNSEEN PHOTOGRAPHY & TEXT FROM WAITE & SMITH

Secrets of the Waite-Smith Tarot
The True Story of the Worlds Most Popular Tarot
Marcus Katz and Tali Goodwin

Uncover the secrets of tarot with never-before-seen material from Waite's own hand, an exploration of the worlds and environments that shaped both Waite and Smith, and a practical guide to interpreting the cards. Drawing on Waite's own words, examples, unpublished materials, and more, this groundbreaking book unlocks the symbols and intentions of the cards.

Secrets of the Waite-Smith Tarot explores the fascinating origins of the most popular tarot system in the world. Explore the comparisons between the court cards and the stage characters that influenced Smith. You'll also learn about Smith's intuitive understanding of the Tree of Life and how that wisdom is reflected in her Minors. This exciting guide will introduce you to a new understanding of the Rider-Waite-Smith deck.

ISBN: 978-0-7387-4119-2 • 7½ x 9⅛ • 480 pp.

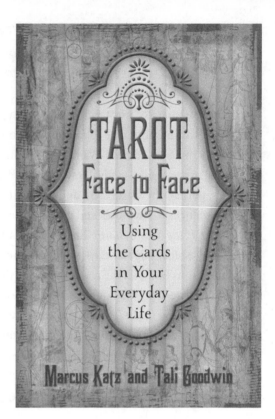

TAROT
Face to Face

Using
the Cards
in Your
Everyday
Life

Marcus Katz and Tali Goodwin

Tarot Face to Face
Using the Cards in Your Everyday Life
MARCUS KATZ AND TALI GOODWIN

Learn the essential skills of tarot reading in everyday practical situations for friends, family, and clients. Authors Marcus Katz and Tali Goodwin offer guidance on how to read with confidence in any face-to-face situation, based on insight from an extensive survey involving hundreds of professional readers who answered questions from real-life clients over a five-year period. With suggestions for what to say and how to say it, and ideas for using tarot in a relationship or as a party game, *Tarot Face to Face* provides spread and interpretation strategies for questions about soul mates, spiritual growth, money, families, careers, and more. Transform querent questions—even those that are tricky or vague—into bold, accurate readings.

ISBN: 978-0-7387-3310-4 • 6 x 9 • 240 pp.

Around the Tarot in 78 Days
A Personal Journey Through the Cards
Marcus Katz and Tali Goodwin

Journey into the exciting world of tarot with this comprehensive 78-day course. Uniquely presented in a card-a-day format, this workbook provides a solid foundation in tarot—and offers new ways to enrich your life using the wisdom of the cards.

Well-known tarot readers and instructors Marcus Katz and Tali Goodwin take you through the symbolic landscape of tarot card by card. Progress through the exercises in sequence or study the cards in whatever order you'd like. Casting traditional interpretation methods in a fresh and modern light, Katz and Goodwin teach you how to interpret spreads by experiencing them as meditations, activities, affirmations, and oracles. Discover the keywords of each card and how to use them. Delve even deeper with gated spreads—a series of spreads guiding you toward a powerful experience—and integrative lessons on magick and kabbalistic correspondences.

ISBN: 978-0-7387-3044-8 • 7½ x 9⅛ • 456 pp.

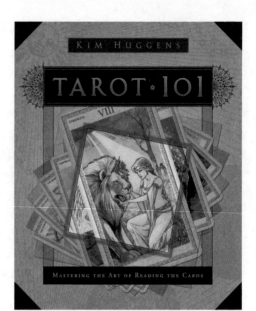

KIM HUGGENS

TAROT · 101

MASTERING THE ART OF READING THE CARDS

Tarot 101
Mastering the Art of Reading the Cards
KIM HUGGENS

Are you eager to learn the tarot in a way that's both effective and fun? This complete course in tarot demystifies the art of card reading by drawing on your intuition and imagination.

Tarot 101 will turn anyone into a professional card reader in just twenty-two practical lessons. Each lesson introduces an essential concept broken down into four topics, with exercises, tips, and key terms, plus optional tasks designed to enhance your learning experience. Unlike other tarot guides, *Tarot 101* groups the cards according to theme—a simpler, more intuitive way to learn—and is compatible with any tarot deck. Learn about all crucial topics, including the history of tarot, methods of interpretation, creating spreads, reversals, card reading ethics, client-reader etiquette, imagery symbolism and divinatory meaning, and developing your intuition for insightful readings.

ISBN: 978-0-7387-1904-7 • 7½ x 9⅛ • 360 pp.